# PREACHING TOOLS

## AN ANNOTATED SURVEY OF COMMENTARIES AND PREACHING RESOURCES FOR EVERY BOOK OF THE BIBLE

# DAVID L. ALLEN

SEMINARY HILL PRESS

Seminary Hill Press
2001 West Seminary Drive
Fort Worth, Texas 76115

*Preaching Tools: An Annotated Survey of Commentaries and Preaching Resources for Every Book of the Bible*
By Allen, David L.
Copyright © 2014 by David L. Allen
ISBN: 978-0-9839392-3-8
Publication Date: June 2014

# CONTENTS

# INTRODUCTION

I have always loved books. When I was called to preach at age 16, a retired minister gave me 400 volumes from his library. Since then, I have been something of a collector of theological books, including hundreds of commentaries. These have served as treasured resources for sermon preparation over the past 40 years in the pulpit.

What I've tried to do in this book is provide an annotated bibliography for preachers of helpful resources, mostly commentaries, for every book of the Bible, in English. Most of the books listed in this bibliography I own in my personal library. These are the works that I have found to be the most helpful in sermon preparation, and just like that retired minister shared with me from his experience, I hope to do so with the next generation of pastors and preachers.

I have made use of a number of sources in compiling my list and annotations. These include the following:

Cyril Barber, *The Minister's Library*, vols. 1 & 2.

Kenneth Barker & Bruce Waltke, *Bibliography for Old Testament Exegesis and Exposition*. 3rd edition, revised.

David Brookman, *Basic Books for the Minister's Library*.

D. A. Carson, *New Testament Commentary Survey*. 7th ed.

Brevard Childs, *Old Testament Books for Pastor and Teacher*.

Frederick Danker, *Multipurpose Tools for Bible Study*.

John Glynn, *Commentary & Reference Survey*.

Joseph Fitzmyer, *An Introductory Bibliography for the Study of Scripture*.

Kregel Press. *A Classic Bible Study Library for Today*.

Tremper Longmann III. *Old Testament Commentary Survey*. 5th ed.

Ralph Martin, *New Testament Books for Pastor and Teacher*.

Douglas Moo, *An Annotated Bibliography on the Bible and the Church*.

Jim Rosscup, *Commentaries for Biblical Expositors*.

David Scholer, *A Basic Bibliographic Guide for New Testament Exegesis*.

Wilbur Smith, *Profitable Bible Study.*

Charles Spurgeon, *Commenting and Commentaries.*

Douglas Stuart, *A Guide to Selecting and Using Bible Commentaries.*

Martha Sugg & John Boone Trotti, eds. *Building a Pastor's Library.*

Warren Wiersbe, *A Basic Library for Bible Students.*

The old saying, "One man's trash is another man's treasure," is certainly true when it comes to commentaries. Some will look at my list and be surprised at what is not there. Others will be surprised at what is there. Space constraints prohibit me from listing every valuable commentary.

What I have attempted to do is to prepare this list with the theologically conservative expository preacher in mind. It seems hardly necessary to point out that the list is representative, not exhaustive.

The Bible is the primary source of study for sermon preparation. If we are to fulfill Paul's mandate to "preach the Word," we must be as conversant with the Scriptures as possible. We are not preaching about the Bible; we are preaching the Bible. Though there is no substitute for the direct study of the primary source, nevertheless, commentaries are indispensable tools of the trade for every preacher to assist in such study. My goal here is to assist you in developing your personal library of specific commentary tools that will stand you in good stead for a lifetime of sermon preparation and preaching. Someone once remarked that he could look at a pastor's library and tell immediately what kind of preacher he was. Your longevity at your church may very well be related to the number and quality of the books on your study shelves.

There are at least five major reasons why preachers should consult commentaries. First, to be blunt, you need help! No one is an expert on the Bible. When it comes to the Bible, the horizons of your knowledge are always the frontiers of your ignorance. Spurgeon spoke of those preachers who talk so much of what the Holy Spirit reveals to them and yet think so little of what He has revealed to others. As Arthur Gossip once said: "The greatest natural genius cannot subsist on its own stock; he who resolves never to ransack any brain but his own will soon be reduced, from mere barrenness, to the poorest of all imitations." To think one can preach without consulting commentaries is the height of ignorance and arrogance.

Second, introductions to commentaries often provide important background information such as authorship, date, recipients, theme, purpose, and outline, which is vital to any preacher who preaches through books of the Bible. Third, commentaries aid the preacher in understanding the meaning of the text, a vital precursor to sermon preparation. Fourth, commentaries provide helpful information that the preacher may use in the actual exposition, illustration, or application of the text during the sermon. Finally, commentaries, especially those of a more devotional nature, warm the heart and feed the soul of the preacher.

Though many commentaries are listed, this is only a fraction of those that could be listed. There are many that did not make the cut. There are several reasons for why such may be the case. First, the simple fact is there are too many good commentaries available to list them all, even though I might recommend most of them. Second, most commentaries of a more theologically liberal persuasion, however well recognized, have not been included. Those that appear do so in spite of their higher critical leanings because I deem them helpful on the technical exegetical side of the equation, and thus of interest to those so inclined. I do not consider these volumes to be invaluable; in fact, I own many of them. Even a stopped clock is right twice a day. However, many works that appeared from the mid-18th century through the end of the 19th century, and beyond, have sold their birthright for a mess of higher-critical pottage. I remember Carl F. H. Henry's three-fold criticism of higher criticism in a chapel sermon back in the 1980s: "First, Higher Criticism is an adolescent science. An adolescent is one who is fascinated by any novel thing that crosses his path. Second, Higher Criticism has a suspect ancestry. Third, Higher Criticism has a very shoddy track record." Third, I may not be familiar enough with a particular volume to know whether I would recommend it. Fourth, I may have simply overlooked or be totally unaware of a worthy volume.

It behooves the reader to recognize that commentators write for a variety of reasons and their books are useful for a variety of reasons. Some commentaries are valuable simply because they present the needed information to understand textual meaning. Others excel in crafting clarity such that complex issues become intelligible. Others provide the invaluable service of lending themselves to the homiletical needs of the preacher. Still others stir and move the heart and soul to love Jesus more and follow him more fully, keeping the preacher's heart warm for Sunday's pulpit work. After all, preaching is not only an intellectual event; it is a spiritual event.

I have included works from various theological and denominational traditions. It is a great mistake to read only your brand of theology or only from within the confines of your own denomination. Hence, you will find in this volume works ranging from Reformed to Arminian, from Baptist to Catholic. The wise preacher will read broadly.

Readers will notice that I have selected a number of volumes from the past that are out of print and sometimes difficult to find. Some of these volumes are now available online. These are books I consider to be very valuable for preaching. They need to be rescued from the undeserved oblivion to which they have been relegated. Many suffer from the mistaken notion if it is old, it is not helpful, and if it is new, it must be true. Nothing could be further from the truth when it comes to commentaries. Granted, many of the older commentaries of a century or more ago have indeed been mercifully buried in the commentary graveyard. They should not be resurrected. But many others have been lost to the modern preacher simply because they are out of print or they are simply unknown by most today. In the digital age, there is much less problem for preachers to locate these resources now, and many of these books are in fact available online awaiting your digital download. If you are like me and enjoy holding the book in your hands, become a frequent customer at every used bookstore in your path, and you will be able to acquire many of these out of print volumes.

Reading a commentary is like panning for gold. You have to sift through lots of dust and sludge to acquire that precious nugget. Sometimes the nugget is a section, a paragraph, or a single sentence. But once discovered, its value in the truth market and the preaching market is priceless.

There are several authors whose place in church history is such that their commentaries, and especially their sermons, should be consulted when time permits. Of course it is true that even among the titans, their commentaries and sermons are not always on the same level of excellence. In order to conserve space, rather than include these names and works throughout the bibliography (unless otherwise noted), I list some of them here, although many more could be listed. Most of the works of these men are now available online.

> John Chrysostom
> Augustine
> Martin Luther
> John Calvin
> Great Puritan Preachers
> John Wesley
> Charles Spurgeon

There are a few commentary series, sermon series, or sermons on books of the Bible that I highly recommend you consult for homiletical purposes. Rather than list them all individually in the bibliography (unless otherwise noted), I list them here, although many more could be listed. Some of the works of these men are now available on computer Bible programs like Logos or are available free online.

> Charles Simeon *Expository Outlines on the Whole Bible*. (Now available online)

Alexander Maclaren, *Expositions of Holy Scripture*. 17 vols. hardback.

G. Campbell Morgan, *The Westminster Pulpit*. 5 vols. hardback.

Martyn Lloyd-Jones. (Acts, Romans, Ephesians, Philippians, 2 Timothy, 2 Peter, 1 John)

James M. Boice. 27 vols. (Genesis, Joshua, Nehemiah, Psalms, Minor Prophets, Matthew, Sermon on the Mount, John, Acts, Romans, Ephesians, Philippians, 1 John)

Kent Hughes, ed. *Preaching the Word Series*. Crossway. Multi-volume; multi-author.

John Phillips. *The John Phillips Commentary Series*, 27 vols. (Genesis, Psalms, Proverbs, Song of Solomon, Daniel, Minor Prophets, all NT books.)

Warren Wiersbe. *Wiersbe Bible Commentary* (or the individual volumes on all the books of the Bible in the "Be" series.)

I've organized this bibliography in the following categories for each book: exegetical commentaries, expositional commentaries, devotional commentaries, special studies, and sermons. For most of the entries, I offer my own personal comments and/or those of others. These comments should be seen for what they are: my opinion and nothing more. As Brevard Childs wittily remarked: "Bristle when a critic says 'unconvincing,' without demonstrating why the adverse position is made. You may be exposed to a cheap shot." I hope I have not taken any.

In today's busy world, most pastors meet themselves coming. As a result, the pressures of the pastorate restrict time for study and sermon preparation. Some pastor's rationalize their lack of study time accordingly. While understandable, I consider such to be inexcusable. You don't have time to study; you make time to study. I challenge you to be a voracious reader. "Reading makes a broad man," said Francis Bacon. It also contributes to helping one do great preaching! Make your acquaintance with some of these authors, as Childs puts it, "on whose creased brows eternity stands written."

May the Lord bless you as you preach His Word!

David L. Allen
*Dean, School of Theology*
*Professor of Preaching*
*George W. Truett Chair of Ministry*
*Director of the Center for Expository Preaching*

# LIST OF ABBREVIATIONS

| | |
|---|---|
| AB | Anchor Bible (G. Chapman/Doubleday) |
| ACCS | Ancient Christian Commentary on Scripture: New Testament (IVP) |
| ACNT | Augsburg Commentary on the New Testament |
| ANTC | Abingdon New Testament Commentary |
| AYB | Anchor Yale Bible |
| B&H | Broadman & Holman |
| BBC | Blackwell Bible Commentary |
| BCOTWP | Baker Commentary on the Old Testament: Wisdom and Psalms |
| BECNT | Baker Exegetical Commentary on the New Testament |
| BHGNT | Baylor Handbook on the Greek New Testament |
| BKC | Bible Knowledge Commentary |
| BNTC | Black's New Testament Commentaries (=HNTC) |
| BSC | Bible Study Commentary |
| BT | Banner of Truth |
| BST | The Bible Speaks Today (IVP/IVP) |
| BTCB | Brazos Theological Commentary on the Bible |
| CB | Century Bible |
| CBC | Cambridge Bible Commentary on the NEB |
| CBSC | Cambridge Bible for Schools and Colleges |
| CC | The Communicator's Commentary |
| CGT | Cambridge Greek Testament |
| CLC | Christian Literature Crusade |
| CNT | Commentaire du Nouveau Testament |
| ConC | Concordia Commentary |
| CUP | Cambridge University Press |
| DSB | Daily Study Bible |
| EB | The Expositor's Bible (S. S. Scranton) |
| EBC | The Expositor's Bible Commentary |
| ECC | Eerdmans Critical Commentary |

| | |
|---|---|
| EGGNT | Exegetical Guide to the Greek New Testament |
| HCOT | Historical Commentary on the Old Testament |
| Hermeneia | Hermeneia: A Critical and Historical Commentary |
| HNTC | Harper's New Testament Commentary (=BNTC) |
| IB | Interpreter's Bible |
| ICC | International Critical Commentary |
| IVP | Inter-Varsity Press/InterVarsity Press |
| IVPNTC | IVP New Testament Commentary |
| NAC | New American Commentary (B&H) |
| NACSBT | New American Commentary Series on Bible and Theology (B&H) |
| NCB | New Century Bible (MMS/Eerdmans) |
| NCBC | New Cambridge Bible Commentary (CUP) |
| NCCS | New Covenant Commentary Series (Wipf & Stock) |
| n.d. | no date |
| NIB | The New Interpreter's Bible (Abingdon) |
| NIBC | New International Biblical Commentary |
| NIC | New International Commentary |
| NICNT | New International Commentary on the New Testament |
| NICOT | New International Commentary on the Old Testament |
| NIGTC | New International Greek Testament Commentary (Paternoster/Eerdmans) |
| NIVAC | NIV Application Commentary (Zondervan) |
| NPC | New Proclamation Commentary |
| NTC | New Testament Commentary |
| NTG | New Testament Guides |
| NTS | New Testament Studies |
| OP | out of print |
| OT | Old Testament |
| OUP | Oxford University Press |
| P&R | Presbyterian & Reformed |
| Paideia | Paideia (Baker Academic) |
| Pelican | Pelican Commentaries |

| | |
|---|---|
| PNTC | Pillar New Testament Commentary (IVP/Eerdmans) |
| ProcC | Proclamation Commentaries |
| PTW | Preaching the Word Commentaries (Crossway) |
| RCS | Reformation Commentary on Scripture |
| REBC | Expositor's Bible Commentary: Revised Edition |
| REC | Reformed Expository Commentary (P&R) |
| repr. | reprint |
| S&H | Smyth & Helwys Commentary |
| SacPag | Sacra Pagina (Liturgical) |
| SGC | Founders Study Guide Commentary Series |
| SHBC | Smith and Helwys Bible Commentary |
| SIL | Summer Institute of Linguistics |
| SNTSMS | Society for New Testament Studies Monograph Series |
| THNTC | Two Horizons New Testament Commentary |
| THOTC | Two Horizons Old Testament Commentary |
| TNTC | Tyndale New Testament Commentaries |
| TOTC | Tyndale Old Testament Commentaries |
| TPC | The Preacher's Commentary Series |
| UBCS | Understanding the Bible Commentary Series (formerly NIBC) |
| UPA | University Press of America |
| WBC | Word Biblical Commentary |
| WCS | Welwyn Commentary Series |
| WEC | Wycliffe Exegetical Commentary |
| WJK | Westminster John Knox |
| ZECNT | Zondervan Exegetical Commentary on the New Testament |

*The*
# OLD
# TESTAMENT

# GENESIS

## EXEGETICAL COMMENTARIES

Delitzsch, Franz. *A New Commentary on Genesis*. 2 vols. Edinburgh, 1888.

> Delitzsch was a German Lutheran theologian and Hebraist. He founded an institution for training missionaries to the Jews. He is the author of numerous works, including his stupendous two volumes on Hebrews and an amazing book entitled Biblical Psychology, originally published in 1869 but reprinted by Baker in 1966. This is the translation of the 5th German edition. Wilbur Smith said it is "in some ways the greatest commentary on Genesis in any language."

Wenham, Gordon. *Genesis*. 2 vols. WBC. Thomas Nelson, 1987.

> Tremper Longman refers to Wenham as one of the finest Old Testament commentators today. If he writes on it, it is worth having. Wenham's Genesis volume will repay careful study and use. David Bauer said it "represents the best of British Evangelical scholarship."

Westermann, Claus. *Genesis 1-11*. Minneapolis: Augsburg, 1984.

> Westermann's commentary on the entire book is published in three volumes. Brevard Childs calls it "much too long winded for anyone except the specialist." True, but it is scholarship par excellence if you want to wade in deep. Another option is to acquire the abridged volume *Genesis: A Practical Commentary*. Text & Interpretation series. Grand Rapids: Eerdmans, 1987.

_____. *Genesis 12–36*. Augsburg, 1985.

> See above.

_____. *Genesis 37–50*. Augsburg, 1986.

> See above.

## EXPOSITORY COMMENTARIES

Bush, George. *Genesis: Notes Critical and Practical, on the Book of Genesis: Designed as a General Help to Biblical Reading and Instruction.* Boston: H. A. Young, 1871. 2 vols.

> This is an older work that is very valuable for preaching, especially for those without knowledge of Hebrew. I recommend you also get his commentaries on Exodus, Leviticus and Numbers if you like what he does with Genesis.

Candlish, Robert. *Studies in Genesis*. Grand Rapids: Kregel, 1979.

> Candlish was a Scottish pastor and theologian known of his preaching eloquence. Spurgeon said of him, he is always "devout, candid, prudent, forcible." Don't miss his excellent volume on 1 John as well. Brookman calls this work on Genesis "a very important classic ... a treasure house of sermon suggestions."

Davis, John. *Paradise to Prison: Studies in Genesis*. Grand Rapids: Baker, 1975.

> Davis incorporates helpful sources from archaeology and ANE studies in this very readable commentary. Helpful for pastors.

Dods, Marcus. *The Book of Genesis*. EB. New York: A. C. Armstrong & Son, 1893.

> Dods was a pastor for 25 years in Glasgow and then a professor. Excellent expository studies/sermons with good application. Still valuable to consult when preaching through Genesis. Dods wrote good volumes on Corinthians and John [2 volumes] in the EB series as well.

Hamilton, Victor. *Genesis*. 2 vols. NICOT, Grand Rapids: Eerdmans, 1990, 1995.

> An excellent treatment. Use with Wenham and Matthews and you can't go wrong.

Leupold, H. C. *Exposition of Genesis*. 2 vols. Grand Rapids: Baker, 1949.

> Expository in nature and easily readable. A must have for all preachers from this Lutheran preacher. Wilbur Smith said it was the most important commentary on Genesis published by an American scholar.

Matthews, Kenneth. *Genesis*. 2 vols. NAC. Nashville: Broadman & Holman, 1996.

> One of the best all-round commentaries on Genesis by a conservative Old Testament scholar who writes with an eye for preaching the text.

Ross, Allen. *Creation and Blessing: A Guide to the Study and Exposition of Genesis*. Grand Rapids: Baker Academic, 1997.

> This volume is a must for preaching Genesis. More than a commentary, it is really a series of expository sermons, outlined according to the structure of the text, and followed by a brief bibliography on each passage. I would never preach through Genesis without this volume. In fact, I recommend owning every volume by Ross if you plan to do expositional preaching on any book in the Old Testament about which he has written.

## DEVOTIONAL COMMENTARIES

Thomas, W. H. Griffith. *Genesis: a Devotional Commentary*. Grand Rapids: Eerdmans, 1946.

Originally published in three volumes. Principal of Wycliffe Hall in Oxford, Thomas' volume is one of the better devotional works on Genesis.

Strachan, James. *Hebrew Ideals in Genesis*. Edinburgh: T. & T. Clark, 2nd ed. revised, 1906.

Warren Wiersbe said, "One of my favorite books, ... every preacher ought to have in his library. ... One of the most valuable studies of Genesis to appear in this century. It has enriched my life and ministry."

## SPECIAL STUDIES

Greidanus, Sidney. *Preaching Christ in Genesis*. Grand Rapids: Eerdmans, 2007.

From the pen of the Professor Emeritus in Homiletics at Calvin Theological Seminary, this work helps you stay on the straight and narrow hermeneutically as you preach Christ from Genesis. A very helpful volume.

Kirk, Thomas. *The Life of Joseph*. Minneapolis: Klock & Klock, 1985 reprint.

"Detail, insight, and homiletical help abounds," says David Brookman.

Taylor, William. *Joseph the Prime Minister*. Grand Rapids: Baker, 1961.

Taylor was an excellent expositor and devotional writer. See also his *Moses: The Law-Giver*, published in the same year by Baker.

## SERMONS

John Chrysostom preached 75 sermons on Genesis.

Fuller, Andrew. *Expository Discourses on the Book of Genesis Interspersed with Practical Reflections*. In The Complete Works of the Rev. Andrew Fuller. Vol. 3. Harrisonburg, VA: Sprinkle Publications, 1988.

Fuller was one of the great pastor-theologians of Baptist history. Here are 58 sermons on Genesis preached at Kettering before 1805. Brevard Childs said he personally found Fuller's Genesis sermons to be close to the text.

# EXODUS

## EXEGETICAL COMMENTARIES

Durham, John. *Exodus*. WBC. Thomas Nelson, 1987.

> Exegetical and helpful on theology. Tremper Longman cautions that you must watch Durham's "casual attitude toward the history of Exodus."

Hamilton, Victor P. *Exodus: An Exegetical Commentary*. Grand Rapids: Baker Academic, 2011.

> Excellent on exegesis and textual meaning. Not much focus on theology.

Houtman, Cornelis. *Exodus*. 4 vols. HCOT. Kampen: Kok Publishing House, 1993, 1996, 2000, 2002. (Vols. 3 & 4 published at Leuven, Belguim: Peeters, 2000, 2002.)

> Oh lá lá! Critical and detailed to the max! Not for the faint of heart, but everything you ever wanted to know about Exodus. Vol. 4 is a supplemental volume providing a subject index, Hebrew words index, and additional bibliography. This is the lengthiest and single most detailed commentary I've ever laid eyes on.

Murphy, James. *A Critical and Exegetical Commentary on the Book of Exodus*. Andover: Warren F. Draper/Boston: W. H. Halliday & Co., 1868. Klock & Klock reprint, 1976.

> A 19th-century Irish Presbyterian, Murphy's work is still valuable despite its age. Sometimes overly detailed on geographical issues.

## EXPOSITORY COMMENTARIES

Brueggemann, Walter. *Exodus*. New Interpreter's Bible Commentary. 1982.

> Brueggemann is not a conservative, but he often has brilliant insight into the text.

Cole, R. Alan. *Exodus*. TOTC. IVP Academic, 2008.

> Virtually all volumes in the TOTC are worth having. Brief, concise, but helpful treatment of Exodus for the expositor.

Enns, Peter. *Exodus*. NIVAC. Grand Rapids: Zondervan, 2000.

> Covers the territory well exegetically, theologically, homiletically, and practically. Longman gives it 5 stars.

Stuart, Douglas K. *Exodus*. NAC. Nashville: Broadman & Holman, 2006.

> An excellent expository volume that deals faithfully with the text from the pen of an evangelical Old Testament scholar.

## DEVOTIONAL COMMENTARIES

Meyer, F. B. *Devotional Commentary on Exodus*. Grand Rapids: Kregel, 1978.

> Leading British Baptist of the 19th century and contemporary of Spurgeon. Excellent application on the life of Moses.

Wagner, George. *Practical Truths from Israel's Wanderings*. London: James Nisbet & Co., 1862.

> Warren Wiersbe said this volume offers "rich veins of gold that others have ignored or neglected."

## SPECIAL STUDIES

Chappell, Clovis G. *Ten Rules for Living*. New York: Abingdon, 1938.

> On the 10 Commandments. Chappell was an imminent Methodist preacher known for his many books of sermons on Bible characters.

Mohler, R. Albert. *Words from the Fire: Hearing the Voice of God from the Ten Commandments*. Chicago: Moody, 2009.

> Excellent analysis with practical application. Connects the 10 Commandments with Christ and the New Testament well. Helpful for the preacher.

Morgan, G. Campbell. *The Ten Commandments*. Eugene, OR: Wipf & Stock, 1999 reprint.

> I think I own every work Morgan wrote. An outstanding expositor, Morgan was the pastor of Westminster Chapel in London until his death in 1944. This brief treatment is vintage Morgan.

Soltau, Henry W. *The Tabernacle, The Priesthood, and the Offerings*. Grand Rapids: Kregel, 1972.

> A classic study with focus on practical application. Spurgeon called it "richly suggestive."

_____. *The Holy Vessels and Furniture of the Tabernacle*. Grand Rapids: Kregel, 1970.

> Companion volume to *The Tabernacle, Priesthood, and Offerings*.

# LEVITICUS

## EXEGETICAL COMMENTARIES

Hartley, John E. *Leviticus*. WBC. Thomas Nelson, 1992.

> Almost 500 pages. Lengthy introductory material and history of interpretation, followed by solid exegetical work.

Milgrom, Jacob. *Leviticus*. 3 vols. AB. New York: Doubleday, 1991.

> Milgrom is an ordained Rabbi and Professor of Hebrew and Bible at the University of California at Berkeley. Considered the top of the line on Leviticus.

## EXPOSITORY COMMENTARIES

Bonar, A. A. *A Commentary on the Book of Leviticus*. Grand Rapids: Zondervan, 1959 reprint.

> A classic volume from an expository/devotional author worthy of your perusal. Bonar was a 19th-century preacher in the free church of Scotland. He was premillennial. Brevard Childs says of him: "Bonar was a very learned scholar deeply immersed in the history of exegesis."

Gane, Roy. *Leviticus, Numbers*. NIVAC. Grand Rapids: Zondervan, 2004.

> Very helpful for the preacher. Expositional with good application.

Kellogg, Samuel H. *The Book of Leviticus*. Minneapolis: Klock & Klock, 1982 reprint.

> Cyril Barber said of this work: "Perhaps the finest exposition of this portion of God's Word ever to come from the pen of man." Doug Moo calls it "a magnificent old classic." It is also the Leviticus volume in *The Expositor's Bible* series.

Kiuchi, Nobuyoshi. *Leviticus*. AOTC. IVP Academic, 2007.

> Some issues, but overall good.

Rooker, Mark F. *Leviticus*. NAC. Nashville: Broadman & Holman, 2000.

> This is a solid volume by a judicious Old Testament scholar, expository in nature, that addresses well not only the text but also the theology of the book.

Ross, Allen. *Holiness to the Lord: a Guide to the Exposition of the Book of Leviticus*. Grand Rapids: Baker Academic, 2002.

Excellent work by an Old Testament scholar designed especially for pastors and teachers who desire to preach expositionally. Excellent outlines and exposition based on text structure, followed by a brief bibliography on each passage. I consider it indispensable if I am preaching through Leviticus.

Tidball, Derek. *The Message of Leviticus: Free to be Holy*. BST. IVP Academic, 2005.

Excellent for use by those without any knowledge of Hebrew.

Wenham, Gordon J. *The Book of Leviticus*. NICOT. Grand Rapids: Eerdmans, 1979.

As with his Genesis volume, this is an excellent expository commentary on Leviticus that seeks to develop theological themes as well.

## SPECIAL STUDIES

Jukes, Andrew. *The Law of the Offerings*. Grand Rapids: Kregel, 1980.

Classic work on the typological significance of the offerings to Christ.

Seiss, Joseph. *Gospel in Leviticus*. Grand Rapids: Kregel, 1981.

Another classic that shows how Leviticus points to Christ.

# NUMBERS

## EXEGETICAL COMMENTARIES

Harrison, R. K. *Numbers*. Grand Rapids: Baker, 1992.

> One of the best exegetical commentaries by a noted conservative Old Testament scholar.

Levine, Baruch. *Numbers 1-20*, and *Numbers 21-36*. 2 vols. AB. New York: doubleday, 1993, 2000.

> Levine is Professor of Bible and Ancient Near Eastern Studies at New York University. This volume ranks as one of the top exegetical commentaries.

Milgrom, J. *Numbers*. JPS Torah Commentary. Jewish Publication Society, 1990.

> Longman calls it a "masterpiece of erudition, ... a careful study of the details and general message of the book."

## EXPOSITORY COMMENTARIES

Ashley, Timothy R. *Numbers*. NICOT. Grand Rapids: Eerdmans, 1993.

> A solid expositional work helpful to any expositor but not much theological analysis.

Cole, R. Dennis. *Numbers*. NAC. Nashville: Broadman & Holman, 2000.

> This expositional volume would be very helpful to pastors, especially in its theological insight. Longman calls it "a substantial, well-written commentary."

Gane, Roy. *Leviticus, Numbers*. NIVAC. Grand Rapids: Zondervan, 2004.

> See under Leviticus.

Wenham, Gordon J. *Numbers*. TOTC. Leicester: IVP Academic, 1981.

> As with the Genesis and Leviticus volume above, this is an excellent treatment of Numbers, especially for pastors.

## DEVOTIONAL COMMENTARIES

Heslop, William G. *Nuggets from Numbers*. Grand Rapids: Kregel, 1975.

> Practical material for the preacher. Heslop wrote a total of eight volumes on various Old Testament books, and all would be homiletically helpful.

Jensen, Irving L. *Numbers: Journey to God's Rest Land*. Chicago: Moody, 1964.

Most helpful in the area of practical application of the text.

# DEUTERONOMY

## EXEGETICAL COMMENTARIES

Tigay, Jeffrey. *Deuteronomy*. JPS Torah Commentary. Philadelphia: Jewish Publication Society, 1996.

> Viewed as one of the key exegetical commentaries. Takes a moderately critical approach to questions of history of composition, according to Longman.

## EXPOSITORY COMMENTARIES

Block, Daniel. *Deuteronomy*. NIVAC. Zondervan, 2012.

> Very good commentary by an excellent Old Testament scholar that deals with the text in an expository manner followed by good application.

Craigie, Peter. *The Book of Deuteronomy*. NICOT. Grand Rapids: Eerdmans, 1976.

> Solid expository commentary by a capable Old Testament scholar that will prove helpful to expository preachers. Provides careful attention to text, context and background.

McConville, J. G. *Deuteronomy*. AOTC. Nottingham: IVP Academic, 2002.

> Excellent Old Testament scholar; more moderate than conservative on authorship and background issues but very helpful on textual analysis.

Merrill, Eugene. *Deuteronomy*. NAC. Nashville: Broadman & Holman, 1994.

> From the pen of the venerable Old Testament scholar at Dallas Theological Seminary, this is an excellent work that treats the text and theology of the book from a solidly conservative standpoint.

Thompson, J. A. *Deuteronomy*. TOTC. IVP Academic, 1974.

> Excellent entry-level commentary from an evangelical writer.

Woods, Edward J. *Deuteronomy*. TOTC. IVP Academic, 2011.

> As with all volumes in this series, Woods succeeds in presenting a non-technical, brief expository treatment of the book that will prove helpful to pastors, especially those without the benefit of Hebrew.

## DEVOTIONAL COMMENTARIES

Cumming, John. *The Book of Deuteronomy*. Minneapolis: Klock & Klock, 1982.

> Cumming (1807-1881) was a Scottish preacher and pastor of National Scottish Church in London. This is a classic reprint of the 1856 edition. Probably the best known of his works. Application rich for preaching.

# JOSHUA

## EXEGETICAL COMMENTARIES

Butler, Trent C. *Joshua*. WBC. Thomas Nelson, 1983.

> Still one of the best exegetically oriented commentaries on Joshua. Moderately conservative.

Chisholm, Robert. *Interpreting the Historical Books* (Grand Rapids: Kregel, 2006).

> Chisholm is Department Chair and Professor of Old Testament Studies at Dallas Theological Seminary. This is a very helpful exegetical work for pastors from the Handbook for Old Testament Exegesis series.

## EXPOSITORY COMMENTARIES

Blaikie, W. G. *The Book of Joshua*. The Expositor's Bible. New York: A. C. Armstrong & Son, 1908.

> Lots of preaching help from this volume! Brevard Childs says it "reflects the best qualities of the Victorian pulpit and can still be useful for sermon preparation."

Davis, Dale Ralph. *Falling Words: Expositions of the Book of Joshua*. Grand Rapids: Baker, 1988.

> Wiersbe said one should read this book if he plans to preach through Joshua.

Davis, John. *Conquest and Crisis*. Grand Rapids: Baker, 1969.

> Summarizes the book well; helpful for pastors.

Hess, R. S. *Joshua*. TOTC. IVP Academic, 1996.

> Longman considers this one of the best volumes in the TOTC series and one of the best on Joshua.

Howard, David M. *Joshua*. NAC. Nashville: Broadman & Holman, 1998.

> Longman calls Howard's volume "one of the best on Joshua."

Hubbard, Robert L. *Joshua*. NIVAC. Grand Rapids: Zondervan, 2009.

> Good on theology and contemporary significance.

Woudstra, M. H. *The Book of Joshua*. NICOT. Grand Rapids: Eerdmans, 1981.

"A conservative commentary of high merit," said Joseph Allison. Good exegesis. Though Woudstra writes from a Reformed perspective, all traditions will benefit from his theological comments.

## DEVOTIONAL COMMENTARIES

Lutzer, Erwin. *Overcoming the Grasshopper Complex*. Victor Books, 1991.

Lutzer is pastor of Moody Church in Chicago and always good for preachers on illustrations and practical application.

Redpath, Alan. *Victorious Christian Living*. London: Pickering & Inglis, 1955.

Excellent devotional studies worthy of the preacher's consideration. Redpath was a pastor of Moody Memorial Church in Chicago and authored several devotional books. Also see Nehemiah below.

# JUDGES

## EXEGETICAL COMMENTARIES

Fausset, A. R. *A Critical and Expository Commentary on the Book of Judges.* London: James Nisbet & Co., 1885.

Barber considers it "one of the finest comprehensive and scholarly treatments for the expositor."

## EXPOSITORY COMMENTARIES

Adar, Zvi. *The Biblical Narrative.* Department of Education & Culture, World Zionist Organization, 1959.

Brevard Childs said, "Both pastor and teacher will find enormous stimulation in Adar's penetrating analysis of the Samson and Abimelech stories."

Block, Daniel. *Judges, Ruth.* NAC. Broadman & Holman, 1999.

A must-have for the preacher. Well-rounded. See on Deuteronomy above.

Boda, Mark J. *Judges.* REBC. Zondervan, 2012.

Covers history, literature and theology very well.

Butler, Trent C. *Judges.* WBC. Thomas Nelson, 2009.

Longman noted Butler's "thorough discussion of all the important issues ... [and] excellent sensitivity to the theological significance of the book."

Davis, Dale Ralph. *Such a Great Salvation: Exposition of the Book of Judges.* Grand Rapids: Baker, 1990.

See on Joshua above.

Kirk, Thomas & John Lang. *Studies in the Book of Judges.* Minneapolis: Klock & Klock, 1983.

Two volumes in one—*Samson: His Life and Work* and *Gideon and the Judges.* Preachers will find much help from this classic volume.

## DEVOTIONAL COMMENTARIES

Wiseman, Luke. *Practical Truths from Judges* [originally published under the title *Men of Faith*]. Grand Rapids: Kregel, 1985.

Wiseman was an early evangelical British Methodist expositor. Spurgeon recommended this work. Wiersbe said it is a classic study that contains "rich veins of gold that others have neglected." Covers Barak, Gideon, Jephthah and Samson.

Wood, Leon. *Distressing Days of the Judges*. Grand Rapids: Zondervan, 1975.

Rosscup considers it one of the most valuable books on the period of the judges and on character sketches of the main judges. Good help for preaching. Strong on practical application.

## SERMONS

Rogers, Richard. *Judges: A Facsimile of the 1615 edition.* Banner of Truth Trust, 1985 reprint.

Rodgers was a Puritan who preached 103 sermons on Judges to his church. The book is almost 1,000 pages long. Though I don't share the soteriology of the Puritans, I love to read them, and my personal library is full of their works.

# RUTH

## EXEGETICAL COMMENTARIES

Bush, Fredrick. *Ruth and Esther*. WBC. Dallas: Word Books, 1996.

Bush provides in-depth treatment, drawing on linguistic principles of discourse analysis. David Bauer calls it "the most detailed, complete, and technical of the major commentaries on these books, and is probably the best overall commentary on Esther." Needs to be supplemented with other works for practical application.

Sasson, J. M. *Ruth: A New Translation with a Philological Commentary and a Formalist/Folklorist Interpretation*. 2nd ed. Sheffield Academic Press, 1989.

Don't let the latter part of this title scare you off of this volume. Excellent on linguistic issues. Exegetical and technical.

## EXPOSITIONAL COMMENTARIES

Barber, Cyril. *Ruth: An Expositional Commentary*. Chicago: Moody Press, 1983.

Excellent, brief but potent treatment of Ruth by a former librarian at Trinity Evangelical and other conservative institutions who knows his way around theological books better than most.

Block, Daniel. *Judges, Ruth*. NAC. Broadman & Holman, 1999.

See above under Deuteronomy & Judges.

Hubbard, Robert L. *The Book of Ruth*. NICOT. Eerdmans, 1998.

One of the best in the NICOT series. Longman said it "demonstrates careful scholarship, a lively writing style, and balanced judgment."

Lawson, George. *Expositions of Ruth and Esther*. Evansville, IN: Sovereign Grace Publishers, 1960.

This was one of Spurgeon's favorites. Watch out for its moralism, however.

## DEVOTIONAL COMMENTARIES

Cox, Samuel. *The Book of Ruth*. London Religious Tract Society, 1922 [originally published in 1876].

This is really two books in one, also containing Thomas Fuller's *Comment on Ruth*. More devotional than expository but of great profit for the preacher.

Heslop, William G. *Rubies from Ruth*. Zondervan, 1944.

Excellent homiletical value.

# 1 & 2 SAMUEL

## EXEGETICAL COMMENTARIES

Anderson, A. A. *2 Samuel*. WBC. Thomas Nelson, 1989.

Moderately critical perspective.

Klein, Ralph W. *1 Samuel*. WBC. Thomas Nelson, 1983.

Solid on philological and text-critical issues. Not much focus on literary and theological issues, according to Longman.

## EXPOSITIONAL COMMENTARIES

Bergen, Robert. *1 & 2 Samuel*. NAC. Nashville: Broadman & Holman, 1996.

Excellent on the discourse analysis of the narrative text.

Blaikie, William. *The First Book of Samuel*. The Expositor's Bible. London: Hodder and Stoughton, 1898. Republished by Klock & Klock, 1982.

"Exceedingly helpful expositions for preachers who want something substantial and satisfying," said Cyril J. Barber. Barber also said this work was one of the finest devotional commentaries ever produced. Childs noted it "follows the narrative closely and has resisted, at least in part, the preacher's tendency to moralize on the text."

Blaikie, William. *The Second Book of Samuel*. The Expositor's Bible. New York: A. C. Armstrong & Son, 1908. Republished by Klock & Klock, 1978.

See Barber's statement above.

Dean, William John and Thomas Kirk. *Studies in First Samuel*. 2 vols in one.

Older work with a focus on the lives of Samuel and Saul. Good on practical application.

Firth, David G. *1 & 2 Samuel*. AOTC. IVP Academic, 2009.

Firth is the general editor of the TOTC. See also his *1 & 2 Samuel: a Kingdom Comes*. Sheffield: Sheffield Phoenix Press, 2013. The latter work is very helpful and is only appx. 100 pages.

Gordon, Robert. *1 & 2 Samuel*. Library of Biblical Interpretation. Grand Rapids: Zondervan, 1988.

Based on the RSV.

Laney, J. Carl. *First & Second Samuel*. Chicago: Moody, 1982.

Short treatment, 132 pages. "There are few volumes on I & II Samuel which could claim to be more helpful on expositional matters," said Jan Sattem.

Merrill, Eugene. "1 & 2 Samuel," *The Bible Knowledge Commentary*, vol. 1, ed. by Walvoord and Zuck. Wheaton: Victor Books, 1983.

Merrill always has a steady hand on the helm. Very helpful, basic expository commentary, especially for those without Hebrew.

Wood, Leon. *Israel's United Monarchy*. Grand Rapids: Baker, 1979.

Barber calls it "excellent."

Youngblood, R. F. "1 & 2 Samuel," *Expositor's Bible Commentary*, vol. 3. Grand Rapids: Zondervan, 2009.

One of the best expository commentaries on the book to be found.

## DEVOTIONAL COMMENTARIES

Redpath, Alan. *The Making of a Man of God*. Grand Rapids: Baker, 2004 reprint.

Excellent devotional studies full of practical application. If Redpath has written on it, I try to read it.

Taylor, William. *David, King of Israel: His Life and its Lessons*. London: Sampson Low, Marston & Co., 1875.

Spurgeon called it "a grand work which should be in every library."

## SPECIAL STUDIES

Blackwood, Andrew W. *Preaching from Samuel*. New York: Abingdon-Cokesbury Press, 1946.

A series of sermons but less helpful than Blaikie.

Krummacher, F. W. *David, the King of Israel*. Edinburgh: T&T Clark/ Minneapolis: Klock & Klock, 1985.

Krummacher was a German conservative evangelical theologian with a  wonderful gifts in creative writing. This work, along with his most famous Elijah the Tishbite and The Suffering Savior are must haves for all pastors. If nothing else, he will warm your heart, but once you start reading him, you will find yourself using some of his material in your sermons.

Lawson, George. *Discourses on the History of David*. Berwick: 1833.

"Here the life of David is piously turned to practical use," Spurgeon said.

Swindoll, Charles. *David: A Man of Passion and Destiny*. Thomas Nelson, 2000.

Excellent work on the life of David that is biblical and practical. Very helpful for all pastors.

# 1 & 2 KINGS

## EXEGETICAL COMMENTARIES

Provan, I. W. *1 and 2 Kings*. UBCS. Baker, 1995.

> Tremper Longman said, "In its perspective and readability, this is certainly the best available commentary on Kings."

## EXPOSITORY COMMENTARIES

Baehr, Karl. *1 and 2 Kings*. Lange's Commentary on the Holy Scriptures.

> Spurgeon said, "It must have cost great effort to make the homiletical part of this volume as good as it is. It is a treasury to the preacher." B. Childs agrees.

Davis, Dale Ralph. *The Wisdom and the Folly – 1 Kings*. Christian Focus, 2002.

_____. *The Power and the Fury – 2 Kings*. Christian Focus, 2005.

Farrar, F. W. *The First Book of Kings*. The Expositor's Bible. New York: A. C. Armstrong & Son, 1908. Reprinted by Klock & Klock, 1981.

> "Valuable expository studies by a great preacher, a profound scholar," said Barber. Farrar was a literary giant in his day. Few had read as broadly as he did. B. Childs called the work "a rich and vigorous exposition." Overlook the occasional liberal tendency.

_____. *The Second Book of Kings*. The Expositor's Bible. New York: A. C. Armstrong & Son, 1908. Reprinted by Klock & Klock, 1981.

> See comments above. Both works would be helpful to the expositor.

House, Paul R. *1, 2 Kings*. NAC. Nashville: Broadman & Holman, 1995.

> A very helpful work for pastors from the pen of a conservative Old Testament scholar. Explains the text and covers theological matters as well.

Kirk, Thomas and George Rawlinson. *Studies in the Books of Kings.* 2 volumes in one. Minneapolis: Klock & Klock, 1983 reprint. [Kirk's volume is *Solomon: His Life and His Works*, and Rawlinson penned *The Lives and Times of the Kings of Israel and Judah*]

> Barber said, "Kirk's handling of the life of Solomon [1 Kings 1–9] is done so well that it suggests messages by the score and provides, in addition, pertinent areas of application." Weigh his chronology against Thiele's *Mysterious Numbers of the Hebrew Kings*, and you can't go wrong with these volumes.

Konkel, A. H. *First and Second Kings.* NIVAC. Zondervan, 2006.

Patterson, Richard D. and Hermann J. Austel. *1 and 2 Kings.* EBC, vol. 4. Frank E. Gaebelein and Richard P. Polcyn, eds. Grand Rapids: Zondervan, 1988.

## DEVOTIONAL COMMENTARIES

Hendricks, Howard. *Elijah.* Chicago: Moody, 1972.

> Expository/devotional messages by a much-loved, well-respected, and gifted communicator who taught for years at Dallas Theological Seminary.

## SPECIAL STUDIES

Edersheim, Alfred. *Practical Truths from Elisha.* Grand Rapids: Kregel, 1984.

> Classic reprint. Solid exposition and spiritual applications.

Krummacher, F. W. *Elijah the Tishbite.* Religious Tract Society, 1836

> Anything from the pen of Krummacher should be in the preacher's library. Study carefully his ability to use descriptive language.

_____. *Elisha: A Prophet for Our Times.* Kregel, 1993.

> See above.

Macduff, John Ross. *Elijah, the Prophet of Fire.* Minneapolis: Klock & Klock, 1985.

> Brookman considers it a must for preachers.

Thiele, Edwin. *The Mysterious Numbers of the Hebrew Kings.* Grand Rapids: Zondervan, 1983.

> This is the first work I turn to when I need to disentangle the chronology of the kings.

# 1 & 2 CHRONICLES

## EXEGETICAL COMMENTARIES

Dillard, R. B. *II Chronicles*. WBC. Nelson/Paternoster, 1987.

Superb in theological analysis and explores connections with the New Testament, according to Longman. Rosscup called it "a gold mine of many details of verse meaning, ... yet be aware of a less than conservative way of handling many things."

## EXPOSITIONAL COMMENTARIES

Barber, Cyril. *1 Chronicles: God's Faithfulness to the People of Judah*. Focus on the Bible. Christian Focus, 2004.

Exposition and application wedded together that many a preacher will find helpful from this master theological bibliographer.

_____. *2 Chronicles: God's Blessing of His Faithful People*. Focus on the Bible. Christian Focus, 2004.

See above.

Bennett, William. *An Exposition of the Books of Chronicles*. Minneapolis: Klock & Klock, 1983.

Older work of value to the preacher. Watch out for the author's higher critical presuppositions at points.

Hill, A. E. *1 and 2 Chronicles*. NIVAC. Zondervan/Hodder & Stoughton, 2003.

Hill sees the book as a sermon.

Japhet, S. *I and II Chronicles*. OTL. Westminster John Knox/SCM, 1993.

Strong in all areas except theology, according to Longman.

McConville, J. G. *I and II Chronicles*. 2 vols. DSB. Westminster John Knox, 1984.

Good exposition coupled with application. Barber said it contains "succinct, pointed comments on each facet of these long-neglected books ... replete with perceptive hints that can be fleshed out with further study."

Wilcock, M. *The Message of Chronicles: One Church, One Faith, One Lord.* BST. IVP Academic, 1987.

Wilcock also sees the book as sermonic in form.

Williamson, H. G. M. *1 and 2 Chronicles.* NCB. Sheffield, 1982.

Rosscup noted that Williamson is good on textual and literary critical issues, but he occasionally finds historical inaccuracies. Generally deals well with the meaning of the text. Useful, but read with caution.

## SPECIAL STUDIES

Von Rad, Gerhard. "The Levitical Sermon in 1 and 2 Chronicles." In *From Genesis to Chronicles: Explorations in Old Testament Theology.* Minneapolis: Fortress Press, 2005.

Childs said the work was "immediately relevant to the homiletical use of the biblical tradition."

# EZRA

## EXEGETICAL COMMENTARIES

Williamson, H. G. M. *Ezra-Nehemiah*. WBC. Nelson/Paternoster, 1985.

Comprehensive. Conservative expositors will benefit but will find some more liberal aspects and speculative reconstructions as well.

## EXPOSITIONAL COMMENTARIES

Clines, D. J. A. *Ezra, Nehemiah, Esther*. NCB. Sheffield, 1984.

Fensham, F. Charles. *Ezra-Nehemiah*. NICOT. Grand Rapids: Eerdmans, 1982.

Donald J. Wiseman said, "The preacher should be sparked by it to many useful lines of thought about the application."

Kidner, Derek. *Ezra and Nehemiah*. TOTC. Downers Grove: IVP Academic, 1979.

Brief but good exposition, as we have come to expect from the pen of Kidner.

Martin, John. "Ezra," *The Bible Knowledge Commentary*, vol. 1. Wheaton: Victor Books, 1985.

Solid expository treatment; especially helpful to those without Hebrew.

Yamauchi, E. M. *Ezra and Nehemiah*. REBC 4. Grand Rapids: Zondervan, 2010.

"One cannot find a better historically-oriented commentary than this one," Longman said.

## DEVOTIONAL COMMENTARIES

Ironside, Henry. *Ezra, Nehemiah, and Esther*. NJ: Loizeaux Brothers, 1979.

Ironside wrote many commentaries, and they are all helpful. Devotional/expository with slight lean toward the former.

# NEHEMIAH

## EXEGETICAL COMMENTARIES

Williamson, Hugh. *Ezra-Nehemiah*. WBC. Nelson/Paternoster, 1985.

See under Ezra.

## EXPOSITORY COMMENTARIES

Barber, Cyril. *Nehemiah*. New York: Loizeaux Brothers, 1976.

See under 1 & 2 Chronicles.

Breneman, Mervin. *Ezra, Nehemiah, Esther*. NAC. Nashville: Broadman & Holman, 1993.

A helpful work. Basic, solid exposition.

Fensham, F. Charles. *Ezra-Nehemiah*. NICOT. Grand Rapids: Eerdmans, 1982.

See under Ezra.

Kidner, Derek. *Ezra and Nehemiah*. TOTC. Downers Grove: IVP Academic, 1979.

See under Ezra.

## DEVOTIONAL COMMENTARIES

Redpath, Alan. *Victorious Christian Service: Studies in the Book of Nehemiah*. Westwood, NJ: Revell, 1958.

Doesn't cover all of Nehemiah, but what it does cover is worthy of reading. Devotional- and application-oriented. Redpath was pastor of Moody Memorial Church in Chicago and authored several devotional books.

Swindoll, Charles. *Hand Me Another Brick*. Nashville: Thomas Nelson, 1978.

Brief exposition with great illustrations and application from one of America's best-known preachers. Preachers can't miss this one.

Lüthi, Walter. *Die Bauleute Gottes; Nehemia, der Prophet im Kampf um den Aufbau der zerstörten Stadt. [The Builders of God, Nehemiah, the Prophet in the Struggle to Build the Destroyed City]* Basel: F. Reinhardt, 1945.

If you're up on your German, these 13 sermons were preached from New Years Eve 1944 to June 1945. They are directed to late and post-WWII Europe. Childs said they "remain powerful expository examples of strong Biblical preaching."

# ESTHER

## EXEGETICAL COMMENTARIES

Bush, Fredrick. *Ruth and Esther*. WBC. Dallas: Word Books, 1996.

> Longman calls this one of the most extensive commentaries written on these books. A bit technical.

## EXPOSITIONAL COMMENTARIES

Baldwin, Joyce G. *Esther*. TOTC. Leicester: IVP Academic, 1984.

> Longman considers this work well-written and based on thorough research. Be aware of Baldwin's problematic statement on p. 24 that some details of Esther "seem improbable." Brief [126 pages], but helpful.

Breneman, Mervin. *Ezra, Nehemiah, Esther*. NAC. Nashville: Broadman & Holman, 1993.

> A helpful work, not bad on the other two books as well.

Jobes, K. *Esther*. NIVAC. Grand Rapids: Zondervan, 1999.

> "Without a doubt this is the best commentary to buy on Esther," Longman says.

Reid, Debra. *Esther*. TOTC. Downers Grove: IVP Academic, 2008.

> Longman considers this volume "brief but helpful exposition."

## DEVOTIONAL COMMENTARIES

Raleigh, Alexander. *Book of Esther: Its Practical Lessons and Dramatic Scenes*. Minneapolis: Klock & Klock, 1980.

> Devotional. "The practical application to life is accomplished with rare skill," Barber said.

# JOB[1]

## EXEGETICAL COMMENTARIES

Clines, D. J. A. *Job 1–20*. WBC. Nashville: Thomas Nelson, 1989.

> First of three volumes. Large volume [1,500 pages plus]. Extensive treatment of linguistic and textual issues. May be a bit more than most pastors want to wade through but generally worth the effort. Consult if you have the time.

_____. *Job 21–37*.

_____. *Job 37–42*.

Seow, C. L. *Job 1–21: Interpretation and Commentary*. Illumination Series. Grand Rapids: Eerdmans, 2013.

> This is probably the top of the line exegetical commentary on Job. Serious expositors should consult it. It will become one of the classics on Job.

## EXPOSITIONAL COMMENTARIES

Andersen, Francis. *Job*. TOTC. Downers Grove: IVP Academic, 1976.

> One of the best expositions in the past 50 years. Verse by verse in approach. David Bauer says it is "among the most substantive and authoritative volumes in the Tyndale series."

Archer, Gleason. *The Book of Job: God's Answer to the Problem of Undeserved Suffering*. Grand Rapids: Baker, 1982.

> Good blend of exposition and application. Helpful for preaching.

Barnes, Albert. *Notes on Job*. 2 vols.

> Spurgeon calls it "exceedingly good; ... the student should purchase this work at once, as it is absolutely necessary to his library."

Davidson, Andrew. *Job*. Cambridge Bible Commentary.

> Childs considered this a "lucid, sober analysis of the literal sense of the text."

---

1 For a helpful bibliography on all matters of interpretation related to Job, consult Peter Enns, *Poetry and Wisdom* (Grand Rapids: Baker, 1997), 74–93.

Gibson, Edgar. *The Book of Job*. Minneapolis: Klock & Klock, 1978 reprint.

First published in 1899, it contains useful outlines, helpful to expository preachers. Good word studies.

Green, William Henry. *The Argument of the Book of Job*. Minneapolis: Klock & Klock, 1981.

"Few works are as helpful as this one in tracing the argument of the book," Barber said.

Hartley, J. E. *The Book of Job*. NICOT. Grand Rapids: Eerdmans, 1988.

Solidly evangelical and well-researched. Rosscup calls it one of the best conservative works on Job. Hartley attempts to canonically connect Job with the rest of the Old Testament.

Longman, Tremper. *Job*. Baker Commentary on the Old Testament: Wisdom and Psalms. Grand Rapids: Baker Academic, 2012.

Longman attempts a theological explanation of Job. Emphasis on place in the canon and relationship to the New Testament.

## DEVOTIONAL COMMENTARIES

Blackwood, Andrew. *A Devotional Introduction to Job*. Grand Rapids: Baker, 1959.

The title says it all.

Caryl, Joseph. *Job: Exposition with Practical Observations*. 12 vols. [Also in abridged form under the title *An Exposition of Job*] Grand Rapids: Kregel.

Puritan treatment in excess! Published between 1644 and 1646. Expositional and devotional. If you have the time, you will find some good nuggets for preaching in the 12 volumes. Otherwise, consult the abridged volume.

Chambers, Oswald. *Baffled to Fight Better*. 4th ed. Oxford: Alden & Co., n.d.

Expository messages on the book by the author of the classic *My Utmost for His Highest*. Mac Brunson said it was especially helpful to him during a difficult time in his ministry.

Cox, Samuel. *Commentary on the Book of Job*. London: C. Kegan Paul and Co., 1880.

Excellent devotional commentary.

Morgan, G. Campbell. *The Answer of Jesus to Job*. Wipf & Stock, 2013 reprint.

> Warren Wiersbe says, "It is so good you will be tempted to preach it." Morgan relates the book to Christ and the New Testament.

Thomas, David. *The Book of Job, Exegetically and Practically Considered*. James & Klock Publishing, 1976 reprint (originally published in 1884).

> This work contains 91 homiletic sketches well worth your consideration in preaching Job.

## SPECIAL STUDIES

Ellison, H. L. *From Tragedy to Triumph: The Message of the Book of Job*. Grand Rapids: Eerdmans, 1958.

> Not a verse-by-verse commentary, but helpful, especially on Job's friends.

Zuck, Roy. *Sitting with Job: Selected Studies on the Book of Job*. Grand Rapids: Baker, 1992.

> This volume contains 34 chapters by scholars on key aspects of the book. Helpful to all who plan to preach through Job.

## SERMONS

Gregory (famous sermons on Job. Childs said it was used by the church for a thousand years.)

Calvin, John. *Sermons from Job*. Grand Rapids: Eerdmans, 1952.

> Calvin preached 159 sermons on Job during the weekdays of 1554-1555! This volume presents 20 of them selected by the translator, Leroy Nixon. See also Calvin's *Sermons on Job*, 751 pages, published by Banner of Truth in 1993.

Spurgeon, Charles. (Spurgeon preached more than 88 sermons on Job).

Chappell, Clovis. *Sermons from Job*. Nashville: Abingdon, 1957.

> See on "10 Commandments" above. Here are 15 textual sermons from the gifted Methodist preacher that will provide good fodder for your sermons.

# PSALMS[2]

## EXEGETICAL COMMENTARIES

Allen, Leslie. *Psalms 101–150*. Revised ed. WBC. Thomas Nelson, 2002.

> Allen's revision of this volume has improved it for contemporary use. One of the best exegetical commentaries.

Craigie, P. C. *Psalms 1–50*. Revised ed. WBC. Thomas Nelson, 2004.

> Best of the modern commentaries on the Psalms on language and Old Testament background, according to Longman. The revised edition incorporates the latest scholarship.

Futato, Mark. *Interpreting the Psalms: An Exegetical Handbook* (Grand Rapids: Kregel, 2007).

> This work in the Handbook for Old Testament Exegesis Series is very valuable to the preacher. Chapter titles include: "Appreciating Poetry," "Viewing the Whole," "Preparing for Interpretation," "Interpreting the Categories," "Proclaiming the Psalms," and "Practicing the Principles."

Goldingay, J. *Psalms*. 3 vols. BCOTWP. Grand Rapids: Baker, 2007, 2008.

> Strong on theology. Longman considers it the best commentary for meaning in original setting.

Perowne, J. J. Stewart. *The Book of Psalms*. Grand Rapids: Zondervan, 1976 reprint [1876].

> Excellent 19th-century commentary from an Anglican Reformed tradition that is strong on exegesis and exposition. This book went through five editions in less than 10 years. It has stood the test of time and is considered a classic in the Evangelical tradition.

Tate, M. *Psalms 51–100*. WBC. Thomas Nelson, 1990.

> Exegetically strong.

## EXPOSITIONAL COMMENTARIES

Alexander, J. A. *The Psalms Translated and Explained*. Grand Rapids: Zondervan, 1975 reprint [1894].

> Weds scholarship with evangelical warmth.

---

2 For annotated bibliographical material on all aspects of Psalms studies prior to 1997, consult Peter Enns, *Poetry and Wisdom* (Grand Rapids: Baker, 1997), 123–147.

Broyles, Craig. *Psalms*. NIBCOT. Hendrickson, 1999.

Clarke, Adam G. *Analytical Studies in the Psalms*. 3rd ed. Grand Rapids: Kregel, 1979.

Outlines, notes and exegetical comments based on the Hebrew text. Each Psalm receives a manageable treatment. Wiersbe said of it: "I only wish I had known about this book earlier in my ministry." Written by one who spent the better part of four years in a Japanese prison camp and house arrest from 1942–1945. The outlines are always alliterated, but there is much help for the expository preacher in this volume.

Kidner, D. *Psalms*. 2 vols. TOTC. InterVarsity, 1973, 1975.

Theological and practical. Brief but very helpful for pastors from the former Warden of Tyndale House in Cambridge.

Grogan, G. *Psalms*. THOTC. Grand Rapids: Eerdmans, 2008.

Strong on theological analysis.

Leupold, H. G. *Exposition of the Psalms*. Grand Rapids: Baker, 1969.

This is one of the best expositional commentaries on Psalms for use by preachers from the pen of a very capable Lutheran amillennialist. Highly recommended. Lengthy, too—more than 1,000 pages!

Maclaren, Alexander. *The Psalms*. The Expositor's Bible. 3 vols. London: Hodder & Stoughton, 1893.

Barber calls this "a masterful treatment." Expositional and devotional. Preachers should consult these volumes when preaching on any Psalm.

Murphy, James. *A Critical and Exegetical Commentary on the Book of Psalms*. Minneapolis: Klock & Klock, 1977 [1876].

See under Exodus.

Phillips, John. *Exploring the Psalms*. 5 vols. Neptune, NJ: Loizeaux Brothers, 1985–88.

Excellent material for preachers. Loaded with outlines, all of which are alliterated, and some of which seem overly forced. Preachers will find excellent illustrations here, some of which were drawn from Phillips' long acquaintance with the writings of F. W. Boreham, and good application. This volume is also devotional in nature and does not necessarily deal with every verse.

Plumer, W. S. *Psalms: A Critical and Expository Commentary with Doctrinal and Practical Remarks*. Edinburgh: Banner of Truth, 1975 reprint [1867].

Plumer was a Southern Presbyterian preacher and writer who taught at Columbia Theological Seminary in South Carolina the last 13 years of his life. Massive volume of more than 1,200 pages, but the title says it all. The Reformed perspective is strong in the doctrinal section, but the exposition and practical sections will provide much thought for sermons.

Ross, Allen P. *A Commentary on the Psalms: Volume 1 (1–41)*. Grand Rapids: Kregel, 2011.

This volume is indispensable when preaching through the Psalms. Excellent exposition plus 150 pages' worth of readable introductory background material, including bibliography.

Spurgeon, Charles. *A Treasury of David*. Peabody, MA: Hendrickson, 2005

Originally a seven-volume set published in 1889 [Spurgeon died in 1892], now available in three volumes. This work will remain a classic on Psalms. Drawing from more than 1,000 authors and sources from every era of Church history and written over a lifetime of ministry, these excellent expositions come with a devotional flavor, coupled with practical application. Spurgeon mainly milks the Puritan tradition on the book but makes his own butter. Chock full of great quotations and illustrations, not to mention other helps for preachers. No preacher who plans to preach on the Psalms can afford to be without this volume. I have consulted it many times since I acquired it as a 16-year-old young preacher from a retired pastor. The great church historian Philip Schaff said of it: "The most important and practical work of the ages on the Psalter. ... It is full of the force of the genius of this celebrated preacher." It can also be found in an abridged volume, but I recommend using the abridgment for devotional reading and stick with the unabridged edition for sermon preparation.[3]

Stott, John. *Selected Psalms and Canticles*. Chicago: Moody Press, 1988 [originally published in 1971].

Excellent expositions by one of the most well-known of British evangelicals. Covers Psalms 1, 8, 15, 16, 19, 22–24, 27, 29, 32, 34, 40, 42–43, 46, 51, 67, 73, 84, 90–91, 95, 98, 100, 103, 104, 121–123, 125, 127, 130–131, 133, 139, 145, 150.

Van Gemeren, W. *Psalms*. REBC 5. Grand Rapids: Zondervan, 2008.

Probably a must for the expository preacher. Longman gives it 5 stars.

---

3 Spurgeon devotes 22 pages to the Psalms in his famous *Commenting and Commentaries*. Every preacher should read every word of those 22 pages to see what Spurgeon says. Originally published in 1876, it demonstrates Spurgeon's breadth of reading and knowledge of commentaries.

Wilson, Gerald. *Psalms*. vol. 1. NIVAC. Grand Rapids: Zondervan, 2002.

This one is also a must for expository preaching with focused application.

## DEVOTIONAL COMMENTARIES

Armerding, Carl. *Psalms in a Minor Key*. Chicago: Moody Press, 1973.

Helpful devotional work on selected Psalms, including many lesser-known Psalms.

Cox, Samuel. *An Exposition of the Songs of Degree*. Minneapolis: Klock & Klock, 1982.

Covering Psalms 120–134, these expositions are well worth your time and investment. Spurgeon called Cox "a great expositor."

Dickson, David. *Psalms*. 2 vols. in 1. Carlisle, PA: Banner of Truth, 1990.

Dickson was a 17th-century Scottish Covenanter whose work on the Psalms is definitely worth looking at. Childs calls this work "warm, vigorous, bold, and devotional." Spurgeon said it was "invaluable to the preacher."

Lockyer, Herbert Sr. *Psalms: A Devotional Commentary*. Grand Rapids: Kregel, 1993.

Called the crowning work of Lockyer's life (he died at the age of 97 and wrote more than 50 books, including the famous "All" series), this volume is a "feast of information and inspiration." Don't miss it!

Olsen, Erling. *Meditations in the Book of Psalms*. New York: Loizeaux Brothers, 1941.

I have used this work in preparing to preach on selected Psalms. Devotional in nature, the author devotes approximately 4–6 pages per Psalm. Lots of practical help for the preacher.

Scroggie, W. Graham. *The Psalms*. 4 vols. Westwood, NJ: Revell, 1965.

Excellent synthetic study of each of the Psalms from the man who taught the great expository preacher and teacher of preachers, Stephen Olford. First rate preaching helps!

## SERMONS

Chappell, Clovis. *Sermons from the Psalms*. Nashville: Cokesbury, 1931.

Textual sermons from the famous Methodist preacher known for his books of sermons on Bible characters.

Donne, John. *Sermons on the Psalms and the Gospels*. Berkeley: University of California Press, 1967.

Donne on the Psalms is worth reading if for nothing else to feed your own soul.

Hubbard, David. *Psalms for All Seasons*. Grand Rapids: Eerdmans, 1971.

Covers Psalms 1, 2, 7, 8, 9, 14, 16, 23, 32, 40, 45, 49, 51.

Jowett, J. H. *Springs in the Desert*. New York: George H. Doran, 1924.

Series of sermons on individual texts in Psalms. Good example of textual preaching. Excellent devotional material.

Manton, Thomas. *Psalm 119*. 3 volumes. Edinburgh: Banner of Truth, 1990 reprint [1680].

Collection of 190 sermons on this Psalm! Rosscup complains that these sermons don't get down to the text enough. I agree. Some devotional value here, though.[4]

## SPECIAL STUDIES

Belcher, Richard P. *The Messiah and the Psalms: Preaching Christ from all the Psalms*. Fearn, Ross-Shire, Scotland: Mentor, 2006.

The title says it all. Helpful volume for preachers. Watch for Belcher to find a Messianic element in every Psalm, a notion that many will struggle with. Reformed perspective.

Bridges, Charles. *Psalm 119: An Exposition*. London: Banner of Truth, 1979.

Brookman calls it "outstanding." Spurgeon said it is "worth its weight in gold." Bridges is also known for his excellent work on Proverbs.

Davis, John. *The Perfect Shepherd: Studies in the Twenty-Third Psalm*. Grand Rapids: Baker, 1980.

Excellent study by a professor of Old Testament and Archaeology. His background information is top notch and extremely helpful for preachers.

Keller, W. Phillip. *A Shepherd Looks at Psalm 23*. Grand Rapids: Zondervan, 1970.

Contemporary treatment of the Psalm that is very helpful to preachers. Good insight on the shepherd imagery.

---

4 Lots of Puritan preaching was done on the Psalms. Consult Henry Ainsworth, Richard Baxter, David Dickson (see above), John Owen, and Richard Sibbs to name some of the more major figures.

Ker, John. *The Psalms in History and Biography*. Edinburgh: Andrew Elliot, 1886.

Fascinating volume on how various people found encouragement from the Psalms. Great illustrative material.

Ketcham, Robert. *I Shall Not Want*. Chicago: Moody, 1953.

Not sermons, but these addresses are "fervent and practical, edifying and enriching," according to Barber.

Longman, Tremper. *How to Read the Psalms*. Downers Grove: InterVarsity, 1988.

Excellent little book for preachers, covering poetry, parallelism, imagery, the different kinds of Psalms, how they were used in Hebrew worship, and their relationship to the rest of the Old Testament.

Maclaren, Alexander. *Life of David as Reflected in His Psalms*. Grand Rapids: Baker, 1955.

Wiersbe calls it "required reading."

Robinson, Haddon. *Psalm Twenty-Three*. Chicago: Moody, 1968.

Good exposition and application for the expository preacher from the dean of evangelical homileticians.

Thirtle, J. W. *The Titles of the Psalms: Their Nature and Meaning Explained*. Popular Edition. London: Morgan & Scott, 1916.

Handy-dandy reference guide by the man who advertised and arranged the sale of 7,000 of Spurgeon's 12,000-volume library to William Jewel College in 1905. Very beneficial to the preacher.

Weatherhead, Leslie. *A Shepherd Remembers: Studies in the Twenty-Third Psalm*. New York: Abington, 1938.

Weatherhead was a liberal Protestant, pastor of City Temple in London. This work on Psalm 23 is very good, and preachers will find these 170 pages helpful. Here is a taste of his wordsmith ability: "The great indictment of what has been called 'the new morality'—a queer phrase because it is not morality, and it is certainly not new—is that it does not work. ... The alleged liberty becomes a crown of lead which 'makes to swoon the aching head that wears it.'"

# PROVERBS[5]

## EXEGETICAL COMMENTARIES

Delitzsch, Franz. *Biblical Commentary on the Proverbs of Solomon*. Charleston, S.C.: BiblioBazaar, 2009.

I try to read anything this conservative German scholar has written, Old or New Testament.

Fox, Michael V. *Proverbs 1–9*. AYBC. New Haven: Yale University Press, 2000.

Perhaps the best exegetical treatment available. Strong exegetical treatment, technical, but from a liberal perspective. Makes extensive use of medieval Hebrew commentaries. Helpful essays at the end of both volumes (see below).

_____. *Proverbs 10–31*. AYBC. New Haven: Yale University Press, 2009.

See above.

Murphy, Roland. *Proverbs*. WBC. Thomas Nelson, 1998.

One of the better exegetical treatments and theological reflections.

## EXPOSITORY COMMENTARIES

Bridges, Charles. *An Exposition of Proverbs*. London: Banner of Truth, 1960 [1846]. Also republished as *A Modern Study in the Book of Proverbs: Charles Bridges' Classic Revised for Today's Reader*. George Santa, ed. Milford, MI: Mott Media, 1978.

A classic work well worth your perusal. The Santa edition is cross-indexed for ease of search. One caution: beware of the moralisms.

Garrett, D. *Proverbs, Ecclesiastes, Song of Solomon*. NAC. Nashville: Broadman, 1993.

Solid exposition. Very helpful to pastors.

Hubbard, D. *Proverbs*. Communicator's Commentary. Dallas: Word, 1989.

One of the stronger volumes in this series. Preachers will find it helpful.

---

5  For annotated bibliographical material on all aspects of Proverbs studies prior to 1997, consult Peter Enns, *Poetry and Wisdom* (Grand Rapids: Baker, 1997), 94–108.

Kidner, D. *Proverbs*. TOTC. InterVarsity, 2008.

Conservative and concise. I always read Kidner when possible.

Lawson, George. *Expositions of Proverbs*. Grand Rapids: Kregel, 1981 reprint.

Lawson, a Scottish preacher and professor of theology of yesteryear, produced a well-balanced expository/devotional commentary. Almost 900 pages of very helpful stuff for the preacher!

Longman, Tremper. *Proverbs*. BCOTWP. Grand Rapids: Baker, 2006.

Very helpful appendix containing essays synthesizing the book's teaching on various subjects.

Phillips, John. *Exploring Proverbs*. John Phillips Commentary Series. 2 vols. Grand Rapids: Kregel, 2002.

Gifted Bible teacher associated with the Moody Bible Institute and the Moody Radio Network. Phillips was very influential in the preaching ministry of Jerry Vines, one of Southern Baptists' most well-known preachers. Though he over-alliterates, many of his outlines are very helpful, and his illustrations are without peer.

Ross, Allen P. *Proverbs*. REBC 6. Grand Rapids: Zondervan, 2008.

Ross always writes with sensitivity to exposition.

Steinmann, A. *Proverbs*. ConC. Concordia Publishing, 2009.

Lengthy introduction, good exposition, with a focus on connecting with Christ and the New Testament.

Waltke, B. *Proverbs 1–15*. NICOT. Grand Rapids: Eerdmans, 2004.

Waltke is a well–known Old Testament scholar who has produced a solid, conservative, exposition of the book. Highly recommended.

_____. *Proverbs 16–31*.

See above.

Wardlaw, Ralph. *Lectures on the Book of Proverbs*. 3 vols. J. S. Wardlaw, ed. Minneapolis: Klock & Klock, 1981.

Spurgeon really liked this volume. You will too.

## DEVOTIONAL COMMENTARIES

Arnot, William. *Studies in Proverbs: Laws from Heaven for Life on Earth*. Grand Rapids: Kregel, 1978.

Wiersbe calls it "a gold mine of spiritual truth."

Draper, James. *Proverbs: Practical Directions for Living*. Wheaton, IL: Tyndale House, 1985.

Excellent treatment of the Proverbs, topically arranged, by a venerable pastor and former president of the SBC. I have used it with profit.

# ECCLESIASTES[6]

## EXEGETICAL COMMENTARIES

Fox, Michael V. *A Time to Tear Down and a Time to Build: a Rereading of Ecclesiastes*. Grand Rapids: Eerdmans, 1999.

Fox is a specialist in the Hebrew Bible, particularly wisdom literature. The book is divided into two main sections. The first half of the book consists of a series of introductory essays on a variety of topics such as the Hebrew word hebel (vanity). The second part is a verse-by-verse commentary and translation of the text. Fox emphasizes lexical meaning coupled with the overall structure of the book. There are problems, but the good outweighs the bad.

Seow, Choon-Leong. *Ecclesiastes*. AYBC. New Haven: Yale University Press, 1997.

Very sturdy volume from an Old Testament Scholar.

## EXPOSITIONAL COMMENTARIES

Bartholomew, Craig G. *Ecclesiastes*. BCOTWP. Grand Rapids: Baker, 2009.

One of the best new commentaries on the book. Expositors will find it helpful.

Enns, Peter. *Ecclesiastes*. THOTC. Grand Rapids: Eerdmans, 2011.

Excellent for preachers.

Garrett, D. *Proverbs, Ecclesiastes, Song of Solomon*. NAC. Nashville: Broadman, 1993.

See above on Proverbs.

Kaiser, Walter. *Ecclesiastes: Total Life*. Chicago: Moody, 1979.

Brief but very helpful. I always look at it when I preach on Ecclesiastes.

Kidner, Derek. *The Message of Ecclesiastes: A Time to Mourn and a Time to Dance*. BST. Downers Grove: InterVarsity, 1976.

Excellent, brief but well-balanced exposition and application. I use it when I preach through Ecclesiastes and always find it helpful.

---

6 For annotated bibliographical material on all aspects of Ecclesiastes studies prior to 1997, consult Peter Enns, *Poetry and Wisdom* (Grand Rapids: Baker, 1997), 52–73.

Leupold, H. C. *Exposition of Ecclesiastes*. Grand Rapids: Baker, 1952.

> Still one of the best evangelical commentaries on the book available. Very helpful for expository preaching.

Longman, Tremper. *Ecclesiastes*. NICOT. Grand Rapids: Eerdmans, 1998.

> Helpful exposition with theological focus. Longman offers his own translation of the book. Rejects Solomonic authorship.

Macdonald, James M. *The Book of Ecclesiastes Explained*. Minneapolis: Klock & Klock, 1982.

> Spurgeon said of it: "Thoroughly exegetical ... to be purchased if found."

Provan, Iain. *Ecclesiastes/Song of Solomon*. NIVAC. Grand Rapids: Zondervan, 2001.

## SERMONS

Hubbard, David. *Ecclesiastes, Song of Solomon*. The Preacher's Commentary. Vol. 16. Nashville: Thomas Nelson, 1991.

> Highly recommended series of messages according to Wiersbe.

Jeremiah, David. *Searching for Heaven on Earth*. Nashville: Thomas Nelson, 2007.

> Good sermons on Ecclesiastes by a well-known expository and radio preacher.

Swindoll, Charles. *Living on the Ragged Edge: Coming to Terms with Reality*. Waco, TX: Word, 1985.

> More a series of sermons on Ecclesiastes than anything, this volume from a seasoned communicator of the Word should be consulted for homiletical wisdom when preaching Ecclesiastes.

Vines, Jerry. Messages on Ecclesiastes on CD.

> Best expository sermon series overall on Ecclesiastes. You really must listen to these messages from the one whom many call the prince of Southern Baptist expository preachers if you plan to preach through the book.

Wardlaw, Ralph. *Exposition of Ecclesiastes*. Minneapolis: Klock & Klock, 1982.

> A series of sermons published in 1868 that would still be helpful to the preacher, especially in the area of practical principles and application.

Young, H. Edwin. *Been There, Done That, Now What?* Nashville: Broadman & Holman, 1994.

Good sermons on Ecclesiastes from the pastor of Second Baptist Church, Houston—one of the largest churches in the U.S.

## SPECIAL STUDIES

Fuhr, Richard Alan. *An Analysis of the Inter-Dependency of the Prominent Motifs within the Book of Qohelet.* Studies in Biblical Literature, vol. 151. New York: Peter Lang, 2013.

This is a very interesting and helpful work by a conservative scholar who teaches at Liberty University. Expositors should consult it in preaching through Ecclesiastes.

# SONG OF SOLOMON[7]

## EXEGETICAL COMMENTARIES

Garrett, Duane & Paul House. *Song of Solomon/Lamentations*. WBC. Thomas Nelson, 2004.

The work of two conservative Old Testament scholars that is beneficial to the pastor.

Ginsburg, C. D. *The Song of Songs and Coheleth*. New York: Ktav, 1970.

One of the top technical commentaries from a Jewish scholar.

Hess, Richard S. *Song of Songs*. BCOTWP. Grand Rapids: Baker Academic, 2005.

A solid work from an expert in Near Eastern background.

## EXPOSITORY COMMENTARIES

Akin, Daniel. *God on Sex: the Creator's Ideas About Love, Intimacy, and Marriage*. Nashville: Broadman & Holman, 2003.

Biblical, practical and tactful. Wonderful treatment based on the Song of Songs that will be useful to any pastor, both personally and in your preaching.

Carr, G. Lloyd. *The Song of Solomon: an Introduction and Commentary*. TOTC. Downers Grove: InterVarsity, 1983.

Good exposition and helpful to the preacher. "Highly recommended," said Bauer.

Garrett, D. *Proverbs, Ecclesiastes, Song of Solomon*. NAC. Nashville: Broadman, 1993.

See above on Proverbs.

Gledhill, Tom. *The Message of the Song of Songs: the Lyrics of Love*. BST. Downers Grove: InterVarsity, 1994.

Longman calls it a model popular commentary; well written and easy to read.

---

7 For annotated bibliographical material on all aspects Song of Solomon studies prior to 1997, consult Peter Enns, *Poetry and Wisdom* (Grand Rapids: Baker, 1997), 148–58.

Glickman, S. Craig. *A Song for Lovers*. Downers Grove: InterVarsity, 1976.

> Literal interpretation of the Song as an expression of romantic love in marriage. Tasteful and helpful.

Longman, Tremper. *Song of Songs*. NICOT. Grand Rapids: Eerdmans, 2001.

> Good on theological focus.

Schwab, George M. *Song of Songs*. REBC 6. Grand Rapids: Zondervan, 2008.

> George Schwab, PhD from Westminster, Associate professor of Old Testament at Erskine Theological Seminary. Solid work, with applicational focus on counseling. Schwab has written a number of articles on Biblical wisdom literature and counseling that pastors will find helpful.

Patterson, Paige. *Song of Songs*. Everyman's Bible Commentary. Chicago: Moody, 1986.

> Very good, brief exposition of the Song that should be in every preacher's library. Excellent survey of the various approaches to the book. Rosscup remarked, "Patterson is lucid and informed in verse-by-verse comment, perceptive about when to be literal and when to be figurative."

Provan, Iain. *Ecclesiastes/Song of Solomon*. NIVAC. Grand Rapids: Zondervan, 2001.

> See above under Ecclesiastes.

## DEVOTIONAL COMMENTARIES

Dillow, Joseph. *Solomon on Sex*. New York: Thomas Nelson, 1977.

> Very helpful work for preachers. Dillow sees the book written by young Solomon describing the love relationship between him and the Shulamite girl. He rightly rejects an allegorical interpretation. Many good applicational things to say about love and marriage, even if all don't come directly from the text. Good resource for pastors.

## SERMONS

Bernard of Clairvaux. *Song of Solomon*. Trans. and ed., Samuel Eales. Minneapolis: Klock & Klock, 1984 reprint.

Bernard was a 12th-century Cistercian monk whose most famous work is his 86 sermons on the Song. He views the book as an allegory of Christ and the church. Though one will find some help in preaching, here is rich devotional material that will feed your soul. Bernard is never commonplace but always imaginative. Barber said this work is "one of the most deeply devotional and spiritually edifying works ever to be written."

Nelson, Tom. *Love Song: A Study of the Song of Solomon*, 1991. (Audio)

Excellent sermons on the Song by a well-known expository preacher at Denton Bible Church in Texas. Appropriate application to husbands and wives. Nelson shows how it ought to be done. Beware of some of the more recent attempts by some younger preachers to preach the Song in a sensational, tasteless way with an overemphasis on sex and employing inappropriate language and content.

Spurgeon, Charles. *The Most Holy Place: Sermons on the Song of Solomon*.

Contains 52 of the 59 sermons Spurgeon preached on the Song of Solomon.

## SPECIAL STUDIES

Bullock, C. Hassell. *An Introduction to the Poetic Books of the Old Testament: The Wisdom and Songs of Israel*. Chicago: Moody, 1979.

One of the best evangelical introductions to the poetical books.

# ISAIAH

## EXEGETICAL COMMENTARIES

Alexander, J. A. *Isaiah: Translated and Explained*. 2 vols. New York: John Wiley, 1851-1852.

> Remains a classic among older commentaries from a Hebrew scholar. Reformed perspective.

Delitzsch, Franz. *Isaiah*. Grand Rapids: Eerdmans, 1976.

> A classic commentary that, though dated, is still of great exegetical value today. Better know your Hebrew for this one! Viewed from an amillennial perspective.

## EXPOSITIONAL COMMENTARIES

Bultema, Harry. *Commentary on Isaiah*. Grand Rapids: Kregel, 1981.

> Bultema pastored Christian Reformed churches until he became persuaded of dispensational premillennialism. Verse by verse and more than 600 pages long, there is much help here for pastors.

Goldingay, J. *Isaiah*. UBCS. Grand Rapids, Baker. 2001.

> Goldingay denies complete Isaianic authorship but offers good exposition.

Grogan, G. *Isaiah*. REBC 6. Grand Rapids: Zondervan, 2008.

> Strongly argues for unity of authorship and strong on theology as well.

Kelly, William. *An Exposition of the Book of Isaiah*. 4th ed. Minneapolis: Klock & Klock, 1979 reprint.

> Premillennial commentary on Isaiah by a man well-versed in eschatology. Barber states it is "well worth the time spent on mastering its contents."

Motyer, J. A. *The Prophecy of Isaiah: an Introduction and Commentary*. Downers Grove: InterVarsity, 1993.

> This is one of the best commentaries on Isaiah that would be most helpful to the expositor. Motyer writes from a Reformed theological perspective.

Oswalt, John N. *Isaiah 1–39*. NICOT. Grand Rapids: Eerdmans, 1986.

> This is a must-have for the expository preacher. Conservative and expositional.

_____. *Isaiah 40–66*. NICOT. Grand Rapids: Eerdmans, 1998.

See above.

_____. *Isaiah*. NIVAC. Grand Rapids: Zondervan, 2003.

Excellent exposition as in his NICOT volumes but here with a specific focus on application. A must-have for the expository preacher.

Smith, George Adam. *The Book of Isaiah*. The Expositor's Bible. 2 vols. London/New York: Harper & Bros., 1927.

Wilbur Smith said Smith's work is "written in elegant style ... pages sparkle with brilliance, and are so suggestive that one preaching on the text he is commentating upon cannot get away from his remarks." But as Smith continues, the volume is "vitiated by his bondage to the theories of the higher critical school, and he does not mind chopping up the text when he feels so inclined." Extract the gold and discard the dross.

Young, E. J. *The Book of Isaiah*. 3 vols. Grand Rapids: Eerdmans, 1965, 1969, 1972.

Although 1,700 pages total, preachers will find lots of help from Young. Solidly conservative. Don't miss his comments on Isaiah 53. Amillennial in perspective.

## DEVOTIONAL COMMENTARIES

Jennings, F. C. *Isaiah*. Neptune, N.J.: Loizeaux Brothers, 1966.

A very fine combination of devotional and expository approach. Plymouth Brethren background. Wilbur Smith recommends him but notes his exposition of some prophecies seem not to be based solidly on the text itself.

## SPECIAL STUDIES

Baron, David. *The Servant of Jehovah*. Grand Rapids: Zondervan, 1954 reprint.

Excellent study of Isaiah 53.

Bock, Darrell, and Mitch Glaser, eds. *The Gospel According to Isaiah 53: Encountering the Suffering Servant in Jewish and Christian Theology*. Grand Rapids: Kregel Academic & Professional, 2012.

Excellent treatment of Isaiah 53 by a bevy of evangelical scholars.

Lindsey, F. Duane. *The Servant Songs: A Study in Isaiah*. Chicago: Moody, 1985.

Excels at showing Christ in the Old Testament. "Preachers will find this volume invaluable," claims Barber.

Meyer, F. B. *Christ in Isaiah*. Fort Washington, PA: Christian Literature Crusade, 1973.

Devotional treatment of Isaiah 40–55 from the pen of a well-loved Baptist pastor, preacher and writer who was a contemporary of Spurgeon. Own anything written by Meyer.

Redpath, Alan. *The Promise of Deliverance*. In Faith for the Times: Studies in the Prophecy of Isaiah 40 to 66. Part 1. Old Tappan, NJ: Fleming Revell, 1972.

I read everything I can get my hands on by this former pastor of Moody Church. Don't enter the pulpit without having read Redpath.

_____. *The Plan of Deliverance*. In Faith for the Times: Studies in the Prophecy of Isaiah 49 to 54. Part II.

See above.

_____. *The Fruit of Deliverance*. In Faith for the Times: Studies in the Prophecy of Isaiah 55-66. Part III.

See above.

## SERMONS

Criswell, W. A. *Isaiah: An Exposition*. Grand Rapids: Zondervan, 1977.

Excellent preaching material from the venerable pastor of FBC Dallas for 50 years.

# JEREMIAH

## EXEGETICAL COMMENTARIES

Lundbom, J. *Jeremiah 1–20*. AYBC. New Haven: Yale University Press, 1999.

Longman gives it 5 stars and says it is a must-buy for scholars and pastors who are really interested in delving into Jeremiah.

_____. *Jeremiah 21–36*. 2004.

See above.

_____. *Jeremiah 37–52*. 2004.

See above.

## EXPOSITIONAL COMMENTARIES

Dearman, J. Andrew. *Jeremiah/Lamentations*. NIVAC. Grand Rapids: Zondervan, 2002.

Helpful exposition and application for the preacher.

Feinberg, Charles. *Jeremiah*. Grand Rapids: Zondervan, 1982.

Detailed exposition, including introductory matters and good bibliography. Premillennial. Also can be found in the Expositor's Bible Commentary. If I were preaching through Jeremiah, I would consult it regularly.

Fretheim, Terence E. *Jeremiah*. SHBC. Macon, GA. Smyth and Helwys, 2002.

Longman gives it 5 stars.

Harrison, R. K. *Jeremiah & Lamentations*. TOTC. Downers Grove: InterVarsity, 2008.

Not a lengthy treatment, but very helpful. Harrison always delivers.

Huey, F. B. *Jeremiah, Lamentations*. NAC. Nashville: Broadman & Holman, 1993.

Good, basic exposition that will be helpful to the preacher.

Laetsch, Theodore. *Jeremiah/Lamentations*. St. Louis: Concordia Publishing House, 1952.

Moo considers it a solid evangelical work from a Lutheran perspective.

Thompson, J. A. *The Book of Jeremiah*. NICOT. 2nd Revised ed. Grand Rapids: Eerdmans, 1980.

This is one all preachers should consult when preaching through Jeremiah.

## DEVOTIONAL COMMENTARIES

Morgan, G. Campbell. *Studies in the Prophecy of Jeremiah*. New York/ Chicago: Fleming Revell, 1931.

A great expository preacher's approach to explaining the book.

# LAMENTATIONS[8]

## EXEGETICAL COMMENTARIES

Hillers, Delbert R. *Lamentations*. Anchor Bible. Garden City, NY: Doubleday, 1972.

Exhaustive, though readable, treatment but from a Neo-orthodox perspective.

## EXPOSITORY COMMENTARIES

Dobbs-Allsopp, F. W. *Lamentations*. Interpretation. Louisville, KY: John Knox Press, 2002.

"Masterfully relates the original message of the book to the theology of the Old Testament as a whole and to contemporary reflection," according to Bauer. Helpful for practical application in preaching.

Ferris, Paul W. *Lamentations*. REBC 7. Grand Rapids: Zondervan, 2010.

Good expositional commentary from one who has focused on this book.

Harrison, R. K. *Jeremiah & Lamentations*. TOTC. Downers Grove: InterVarsity, 2008.

See above.

Huey, F. B. *Jeremiah, Lamentations*. NAC. Nashville: Broadman & Holman, 1993.

See Jeremiah above.

Parry, R. A. *Lamentations*. THOTC. Grand Rapids: Eerdmans, 2010.

Longman calls this a "wonderful resource for preachers."

## SPECIAL STUDIES

Kaiser, Walter. *Grief and Pain in the Plan of God*. Fearn: Christian Focus, 2004. Formerly published as *A Biblical Approach to Personal Suffering*. Chicago: Moody, 1982.

Very helpful little volume from the former president of Gordon-Conwell Seminary. Kaiser always has something good to offer the preacher. This is no exception.

---

8  For annotated bibliographical material on all aspects of Lamentations studies prior to 1997, consult Peter Enns, *Poetry and Wisdom* (Grand Rapids: Baker, 1997), 159–63.

# EZEKIEL

## EXEGETICAL COMMENTARIES

Greenberg, M. *Ezekiel 1–20*. AYBC. New Haven: Yale University Press, 1983.

> Many consider Greenberg to be the foremost authority on Ezekiel. Ph.D., He was Professor of Biblical Studies at Hebrew University in Jerusalem, prolific author, and served as editor of the Encyclopaedia Judaica. He offers a translation that incorporates the subtleties of the Hebrew text. You won't agree with everything, but this work is top notch.

_____. *Ezekiel 21–37*. AYBC. New Haven: Yale University Press, 1995.

Zimmerli, Walther. *Ezekiel*. Hermeneia. Philadelphia: Fortress, 1979.

> Technical treatment of Ezekiel. Moo considers it the "best liberal book on the topic with good bibliographic information."

## EXPOSITORY COMMENTARIES

Alexander, Ralph H. *Ezekiel*. REBC 7. Grand Rapids: Zondervan, 2010.

> Solid exposition from a premillennial perspective. Very helpful.

Block, Daniel. *The Book of Ezekiel 1–24*. NICOT. Grand Rapids: Eerdmans, 1997.

> This is a must-have commentary for all scholars and preachers. Solidly conservative. Don't head to the pulpit without having consulted this one.

_____. *The Book of Ezekiel 25–48*. 1998.

> See above.

Cooper, Lamar. *Ezekiel*. NAC. Nashville: Broadman & Holman, 1994.

> This work is very helpful to the preacher. Solidly expositional but not tedious. Don't miss his analysis of Ezekiel 40–48.

Craigie, P. *Ezekiel*. DSB. Philadelphia: Westminster, 1983.

> Conservative, evangelical exposition.

Duguid, Iain M. *Ezekiel*. NIVAC. Grand Rapids: Zondervan, 1999.

> Excellent exposition and application for the pastor. Longman gives it 5 stars. Reformed perspective.

Fairbairn, Patrick. *An Exposition of Ezekiel*. Grand Rapids: Zondervan, 1960. Published under the same title: Minneapolis: Klock & Klock, 1979 [1851].

Thorough, readable, evangelical. Especially helpful on chapters 40–48.

Feinberg, Charles. *The Prophecy of Ezekiel*. Chicago: Moody, 1969.

Excellent premillennial treatment of the book. Chapter-by-chapter approach. Accepts chapters 40–48 as speaking of a literal rebuilt temple in the millennium.

Stuart, Douglas. *Ezekiel*. The Preacher's Commentary. Thomas Nelson, 1989.

Solid exposition that would be very helpful to all preachers.

## DEVOTIONAL COMMENTARIES

Blackwood, Andrew W. *The Other Son of Man*. Grand Rapids: Baker, 1966.

Blackwood was a Presbyterian pastor. This work covers the "Son of Man" concept in Ezekiel as related to Christ. It is really a series of 12 sermons on key passages in the book. Don't miss the Foreword for a helpful survey of the "Son of Man" concept. Blackwood also wrote a 250 page verse by verse commentary on Ezekiel that preachers would find helpful entitled Ezekiel: Prophecy of Hope (Grand Rapids: Baker, 1965).

Guthrie, Thomas. *The Gospel in Ezekiel*. Grand Rapids: Zondervan, n.d. reprint.

Contains 22 studies in 400 pages over aspects of Ezekiel applying a Reformed understanding of the Christian life via connection with the New Testament. Wordy but helpful material.

# DANIEL

## EXEGETICAL COMMENTARIES

Goldingay, John. *Daniel*. WBC. Waco, TX: Word, 1989.

> Too much form criticism for my taste, and Goldingay doesn't think the book is entirely historical. However, it can be exegetically helpful.

## EXPOSITORY COMMENTARIES

Baldwin, Joyce G. *Daniel*. TOTC. Downers Grove: InterVarsity, 2008.

> As we have come to expect from authors in this series, this is a solid, conservative work helpful to the preacher.

Hill, Andrew E. *Daniel*. REBC 8. Grand Rapids: Zondervan, 2008.

> Conservative exposition that would be helpful to all who preach from Daniel.

Longman, Tremper. *Daniel*. NIVAC. Grand Rapids: Zondervan, 1999.

> A good work from the perspective of practical application to today's world. Not so good on the last six chapters. Longman's Covenant theology causes him to miss the correct interpretation of Daniel's prophetic section in my judgment.

Miller, Stephen R. *Daniel*. NAC. Nashville: Broadman & Holman, 1994.

> Conservative approach to Daniel. Helpful for expositors.

Wallace, Ronald S. *The Lord is King: the Message of Daniel*. BST. Downers Grove: InterVarsity, 1979.

> Another good conservative work on Daniel helpful for expositors. "Outstanding book on the topic," says Moo.

Walvoord, John. *Daniel: the Key to Prophetic Revelation*. Chicago: Moody, 1971.

> Written to be a companion volume to his excellent commentary on Revelation, this work by a premillennial specialist is an excellent verse-by-verse treatment. Even if you are not a premillenialist, this is one you must have in your library.

Wood, Leon. *A Commentary on Daniel*. Grand Rapids: Zondervan, 1973.

> Excellent verse-by-verse commentary on Daniel. Very helpful for expository preaching through the book. Premillennial in perspective.

## SPECIAL STUDIES

Anderson, Robert. *The Coming Prince*. London: Hodder & Stoughton, 1909.

Excellent study of Daniel 9 by a premillenialist.

Wilson, Robert Dick. *Studies in the Book of Daniel*. 2 vols. in one. Grand Rapids: Baker, 1972 reprint.

A must-read for defending Daniel against the critics from the W. H. Green Professor of Semitic Languages and Old Testament Criticism at Princeton Theological Seminary. Contains 688 pages of superb scholarship!

## SERMONS

Criswell, W. A. *Expository Sermons on Daniel*. 4 vols. Grand Rapids: Zondervan, 1972.

One of Criswell's best books. A series of sermons preached at FBC Dallas. Premillennial perspective.

Greidanus, Sidney. *Preaching Christ from Daniel: Foundations for Expository Sermons*. Grand Rapids: Eerdmans, 2012.

Phillips, John & Jerry Vines. *Exploring the Book of Daniel*. Neptune, NJ: Loizeaux Brothers, 1990.

Valuable sermons, including outlines, brief exposition, illustration and application. Dispensational perspective.

# THE MINOR PROPHETS

*Several single or multi-volume sets treat all the Minor Prophets.*
*I recommend the following.*

Feinberg, Charles Lee. *The Minor Prophets*. Chicago: Moody, 1976.

> This is a one-volume edition of what was originally published in five volumes. Feinberg was raised in an orthodox Jewish home and studied Hebrew and related subjects for 14 years in preparation for the rabbinate. Excellent resource for the expository preacher. No footnotes. The book is a blend of exposition and devotion.

Freeman, Hobart. *An Introduction to the Old Testament Prophets*. Chicago: Moody, 1968.

> Excellent introduction for the pastor.

Henderson, Ebenezer. *The Twelve Minor Prophets*. Grand Rapids: Baker, 1980 reprint [1845].

> This is an exegetical commentary written by a Scottish scholar who studied under Robert Haldane and served 20 years as a missionary in northern Europe and then Professor of Theology and Biblical Literature from 1830–1850. Conservative. No easy read but still worth the effort in my opinion, although Childs thinks the volume can be "safely disregarded" due to its "antiquated data."

Keil, C. F. *The Twelve Minor Prophets*. J. Martin, trans. Vol. 2. Edinburgh: T.&T. Clark, 1889.

> Conservative, exegetical and expositional but with a spiritual eye toward the things of God.

McComiskey, Thomas E. *The Minor Prophets*. 3 volumes. Grand Rapids: Baker, 1992, 1993, 1998.

> Each book is treated by a different author. This work is a must for studies in the Minor Prophets.

Pusey, E. B. *The Minor Prophets: A Commentary Explanatory and Practical*. 2 vols. Grand Rapids: Baker, 1961.

> "An extensive and exhaustive study of the Minor Prophets containing homiletical material," according to Barber. Lots of Patristic and Medieval commentary references. Amillennial perspective.

Robinson, George. *The Twelve Minor Prophets*. Grand Rapids: Baker, 1978 reprint [1926].

> Wiersbe calls it "a classic."

Tatford, Frederick. *The Minor Prophets*. 3 vols. Minneapolis: Klock & Klock, 1982.

Masterful exposition, according to Barber. Tatford was a specialist on the Minor Prophets. Premillennial perspective.

## PREACHING THE MINOR PROPHETS

Achtemeier, Elizabeth. *Preaching From the Minor Prophets*. Grand Rapids: Eerdmans, 1998.

Achtemeier actually wrote commentaries on all the Minor Prophets. For each book, she provides a recommended list of commentaries (mostly moderate to liberal in orientation); addresses historical and theological context; then chooses selected texts covering briefly linguistic and rhetorical features, suggested sermon titles, and homiletical exposition. Excellent application ideas for preaching.

# HOSEA

## EXEGETICAL COMMENTARIES

Stuart, Douglas. *Hosea–Jonah*. WBC. Dallas: Word, 1987.

> One of the best on the Minor Prophets, according to Longman. A must-buy for all who preach. Amillennial perspective.

## EXPOSITORY COMMENTARIES

Carroll, Rodas, & M. Daniel. *Hosea*. REBC 8. Grand Rapids: Zondervan, 2008.

> Very helpful work from a trustworthy series. This takes the place of Leon Wood's 1985 "Hosea" in the same series, which is also worth your time.

Dearman, J. Andrew. *The Book of Hosea*. NICOT. Grand Rapids: Eerdmans, 2010.

> Longman gives it 5 stars.

Feinberg, Charles Lee. *Hosea: God's Love for Israel*. New York: American Board of Missions to the Jews, 1947.

> See above, under "The Minor Prophets."

Garrett, Duane. *Hosea and Joel*. NAC. Nashville: Broadman & Holman, 1996.

> Excellent treatment by a conservative scholar. Buy it.

Hubbard, D. A. *Hosea*. TOTC. Downers Grove: InterVarsity, 2008.

> As with the Tyndale series, it is conservative and concise. Longman gives it 4 stars.

Kidner, Derek. *The Message of Hosea: Love to the Loveless*. BST. Downers Grove: InterVarsity, 1981.

> Scholarship, pastoral insight, and a concise writing style. Very helpful.

McComiskey, Thomas. "Hosea." *The Minor Prophets: An Exegetical and Expository Commentary*. Thomas McComiskey, ed. Vol. 1. Grand Rapids: Baker, 1992.

> Longman considers it a must for serious study of the book.

Smith, Gary. *Hosea, Amos, Micah*. NIVAC. Grand Rapids: Zondervan, 2001.

> Exposition and application that will aid the expositor.

Sibbes, Richard. *The Returning Backslider, or a Commentary on Hosea XIV*. Evansville, IN: Sovereign Grace Book Club, 1957. Also in vol. 2 of *Works of Richard Sibbes*, published by Banner of Truth.

"The heavenly Doctor Sibbes" as he was called was probably the most significant of the great Puritan preachers of Cambridge and is always worth reading. This is his commentary on Hosea 14.

# JOEL

## EXEGETICAL COMMENTARIES

Stuart, Douglas. *Hosea-Jonah*. WBC. Dallas: Word, 1987.

> See under Hosea.

## EXPOSITIONAL COMMENTARIES

Allen, Leslie. *The Books of Joel, Obadiah, Jonah, and Micah*. NICOT. Grand Rapids: Eerdmans, 1976.

> Moo considers this work excellent both in scholarship and homiletical value.

Baker, David W. *Joel, Obadiah, Malachi*. NIVAC. Grand Rapids: Zondervan, 2006.

> True to the intent of this series, Baker delivers a satisfying exposition and application.

Dillard, Raymond B. "Joel." *The Minor Prophets: An Exegetical and Expository Commentary*. Thomas McComiskey, ed. Vol. 1. Grand Rapids: Baker, 1992.

> Longman gives it 5 stars. He says, "If you get only one commentary on Joel, this should be it."

Driver, S. R. *The Books of Joel and Amos*. Cambridge Bible. Revised ed. Cambridge: Cambridge University Press, 1915.

> A "tightly packed classic" according to Childs.

Feinberg, Charles Lee. *Joel, Amos and Obadiah*. New York: American Board of Missions to the Jews, 1948.

> See under "The Minor Prophets."

Finley, T. J. *Joel, Amos, Obadiah*. WEC. Chicago: Moody, 1990.

> Covers all aspects of the book well. Premillennial perspective. Longman gives it 4 stars.

Garrett, Duane. *Hosea and Joel*. NAC. Nashville: Broadman & Holman, 1996.

> Excellent exposition from a conservative scholar. Pastors should consult this one.

Hubbard, D. A. *Joel & Amos*. TOTC. Downers Grove: InterVarsity, 2008.

The Tyndale series always delivers good exposition concisely for the pastor.

Morgan, G. Campbell. *Hosea: The Heart and Holiness of God*. Westwood, NJ: Fleming Revell, 1934.

Often considered one of Morgan's finest expositions.

Patterson, Richard. *Joel*. REBC 8. Grand Rapids: Zondervan, 2008.

Scholarly and conservative treatment; very helpful to pastors.

# AMOS[9]

## EXEGETICAL COMMENTARIES

Andersen, Francis I. and David N. Freedman. *Amos*. AYBC. New Haven: Yale University Press, 1989.

A must for those wanting to delve into the Hebrew text, according to Longman, who gives it 5 stars, but watch out for some higher-critical conclusions.

Cripps, Richard. *A Critical and Exegetical Commentary on the Book of Amos*. London: S.P.C.K., 1921. Revised in 1955 by S.P.C.K. Also published by Klock & Klock 1981 reprint.

Solid exegetical study with application as well from a man who taught for many years in St. John's College, Cambridge. Childs is unnecessarily critical to suggest this work can be "safely ignored."

Paul, Shalom. *Amos*. Hermeneia. Minneapolis: Fortress Press, 1991.

Strong on linguistic analysis; not so much on theology. Some higher criticism at work. Otherwise, very helpful. Glynn considers it a "magisterial work, ... impressively thorough."

Stuart, Douglas. *Hosea-Jonah*. WBC. Dallas: Word, 1987.

See above under Hosea.

## EXPOSITORY COMMENTARIES

Allen, Leslie. *The Books of Joel, Obadiah, Jonah, and Micah*. NICOT. Grand Rapids: Eerdmans, 1976.

See above under Joel.

Feinberg, Charles Lee. *Joel, Amos and Obadiah*. New York: American Board of Missions to the Jews, 1948.

See under "The Minor Prophets."

---

9  For annotated bibliography on all aspects of Amos studies, consult M. Daniel Carroll R. *Amos: The Prophet & His Oracles* (Louisville: Westminster/John Knox, 2002). This volume can't be beat for its survey treatment of Amos scholarship through the 20th century. See also Gerhard Hasel, *Understanding the Book of Amos: Basic Issues in the Current Interpretations* (Grand Rapids: Baker, 1991). Hasel surveys the scholarly work on Amos from 1960–1990. The work includes a bibliography of more than 800 works.

Hubbard, D. A. *Joel & Amos*. TOTC. Downers Grove: InterVarsity, 2008.

See under Joel.

Longman, Tremper and Thomas McComiskey. *Amos*. REBC 8. Grand Rapids: Zondervan, 2009.

Updated version of McComiskey by Longman.

Niehaus, Jeffrey. "Amos." *The Minor Prophets*, ed. Thomas McComiskey. Grand Rapids: Baker, 2009.

Good treatment from a solid historical background.

Smith, Billy and Frank Page. *Amos, Obadiah, and Jonah*. NAC. Nashville: Broadman & Holman, 1995.

A basic, workmanlike, treatment helpful to pastors.

Smith, Gary. *Hosea, Amos, Micah*. NIVAC. Grand Rapids: Zondervan, 2001.

True to the series' purpose, this volume delivers helpful application ideas for preaching.

_____. *Amos: A Commentary*. 2nd ed. Mentor Commentaries. Fearn: Mentor, 1998.

Almost 400 pages. Good exposition followed by theological interpretation. This volume is an update of the 1989 Zondervan edition. According to Glynn, it includes socio-rhetorical insights.

Thorogood, Bernard. *A Guide to the Book of Amos*. London: S.P.C.K., 1971.

Left-wing evangelical, strong on application ... a good tool for the pastor, according to Moo.

# OBADIAH

## EXEGETICAL COMMENTARIES

Raabe, Paul R. *Obadiah*. AYBC. New Haven: Yale University Press, 1996.

Longman gives it 5 stars. Highly recommended by David Bauer.

Stuart, Douglas. *Hosea-Jonah*. WBC. Dallas: Word, 1987.

See under Hosea.

## EXPOSITORY COMMENTARIES

Alexander, Baker & Bruce Waltke. *Obadiah, Jonah, Micah*. TOTC. InterVarsity, 2008.

Brief but helpful exposition from the dependable TOTC series.

Allen, Leslie. *The Books of Joel, Obadiah, Jonah, and Micah*. NICOT. Grand Rapids: Eerdmans, 1976.

See above on Joel.

Armerding, Carl. *Obadiah*. REBC 8. Grand Rapids: Zondervan, 2008.

Longman gives it 4 stars.

Baker, David W. *Joel, Obadiah, Malachi*. NIVAC. Grand Rapids: Zondervan, 2006.

Helpful exposition and application ideas for preaching.

Feinberg, Charles. *Joel, Amos and Obadiah*. New York: American Board of Missions to the Jews, 1948.

See under "The Minor Prophets" above.

Marbury, Edward. *Obadiah and Habakkuk*. Minneapolis: Klock & Klock, 1979 reprint [1649–1650 in separate volumes/reprinted 1865 in one volume].

17th-century London pastor. Spurgeon said of Marbury on Habakkuk: he "holds the field among the old English authors, and he does so worthily."

Niehaus, Jeffery. "Obadiah." *The Minor Prophets*. Vol. 2. Thomas McComiskey, ed. Grand Rapids: Baker, 2009.

See under McComiskey in "Minor Prophets"

Smith, Billy and Frank Page. *Amos, Obadiah, and Jonah*. NAC. Nashville: Broadman & Holman, 1995.

See under Amos above.

# JONAH

## EXEGETICAL COMMENTARIES

Sasson, Jack. *Jonah*. AB. New York: Doubleday, 1990.

> Bauer says it is the most detailed and comprehensive analysis available. It is a meticulous interpretation of each verse.

Stuart, Douglas. *Hosea-Jonah*. WBC. Dallas: Word, 1987.

> See above under Hosea.

## EXPOSITORY COMMENTARIES

Alexander, T. D., David Baker & B. Waltke, *Obadiah, Jonah, Micah*. TOTC. Downers Grove:

InterVarsity, 2008.

Allen, Leslie. *The Books of Joel, Obadiah, Jonah, and Micah*. NICOT. Grand Rapids: Eerdmans, 1976.

> See above on Joel.

Baldwin, Joyce. "Jonah." *The Minor Prophets*. Thomas McComiskey, ed. Grand Rapids: Baker, 2009.

> See under McComiskey in "Minor Prophets"

Bruckner, James. *Jonah, Nahum, Habakkuk, Zephaniah*. NIVAC. Grand Rapids: Zondervan, 2004.

> Helpful basic exposition and application for preachers.

Burn, Samuel. *The Prophet Jonah*. Minneapolis: Klock & Klock, 1981 reprint.

> Barber considers it one of the best for preachers.

Feinberg, Charles Lee. *Jonah: God's Love for all Nations*. New York: American Board of Missions to the Jews, 1951.

> Brief but valuable, according to Barber.

Fretheim, Terence. *The Message of Jonah: A Theological Commentary*. Minneapolis: Augsburg, 1977.

> Moderately conservative but a good theological analysis. A helpful volume for preaching Jonah.

Smith, Billy and Frank Page. *Amos, Obadiah, and Jonah*. NAC. Nashville: Broadman & Holman, 1995.

See under Amos above.

Walton, John. *Jonah*. REBC 8. Grand Rapids: Zondervan, 2008.

Exegetical sensitivity, according to Longman.

## DEVOTIONAL COMMENTARIES

Banks, William. *Jonah: The Reluctant Prophet*. Chicago: Moody, 1966.

Barber says Banks "blends historic data with Hebrew word studies and a devotional emphasis."

Exell, Joseph. *Practical Truths from Jonah*. Grand Rapids: Kregel, 1982 reprint [1874].

This book qualifies as an expositional commentary since the author works his way through the book verse by verse explaining the meaning of the text. However, his focus is on application, which makes this a very helpful volume for the preacher. Wiersbe says it contains "rich veins of gold that others have ignored or neglected." Exell was the compiler of the massive, multi-volume *Biblical Illustrator* and edited both *The Pulpit Commentary* and the *Preacher's Homiletical Commentary*.

Fairbairn, Patrick. *Jonah: His Life, Character, and Mission*. Grand Rapids: Kregel, 1964.

When this work had been in print for more than 50 years, Spurgeon called it "by far the ablest English treatise on this subject." It qualifies as an expository commentary as well.

Ferguson, Sinclair. *Man Overboard: The Story of Jonah*. Edinburgh: Banner of Truth, 2008.

Helpful preaching material from this Reformed pastor and former professor of Systematic Theology at Redeemer Seminary in Dallas.

Kirk, Thomas. *Jonah: His Life and Mission*. Minneapolis: Klock & Klock, 1983.

This work will repay the preacher many times over who reads it. Don't miss Kirk's two appendices at the end where he critiques the parabolic view of the book and argues for Jonah as an eighth-century prophet and author of the book that bears his name.
Martin, Hugh. The Prophet Jonah: His Character and Mission to Nineveh. London: Banner of Truth, 1958 reprint. Martin was a Scottish preacher in the middle of the 19th century. An excellent devotional work. Spurgeon said of it: "No one who has it will need any other."

## SERMONS

Hooper, John, "An Oversight and Deliberation upon The Holy Prophet Jonah; made and uttered before the King's majesty, and his most honourable council, by John Hooper, in Lent last past: comprehended in seven sermons, A.D. 1550," Writings of Dr. John Hooper, vol. 5 in the set, *The British Reformers*, pp. 83–192.

## SPECIAL STUDIES

Overduin, Jan. *Adventures of a Deserter*. Grand Rapids: Eerdmans, 1965.

English translation of a Dutch work by a pulpit orator well-known in his day. During the German occupation of the Netherlands, Overduin spent time in four prisons and two concentration camps, including Dachau. He views Jonah as having a style and tone "of an extended, beautifully realized sermon." Preachers looking for insight and help with descriptive language in a sermon will find plenty here!

# MICAH

## EXEGETICAL COMMENTARIES

Andersen, Francis, and David N. Freeman. *Micah*. AB. New York: Doubleday, 2000.

Strong work on literary and linguistic analysis within context. The authors are much less interested in historical and theological issues. Highly recommended by Bauer.

## EXPOSITORY COMMENTARIES

Alexander, T. D., David Baker & B. Waltke, *Obadiah, Jonah, Micah*. TOTC. Downers Grove: InterVarsity, 2008.

See above under Obadiah.

Allen, Leslie. *The Books of Joel, Obadiah, Jonah, and Micah*. NICOT. Grand Rapids: Eerdmans, 1976.

See above under Obadiah.

Barker, Ken and Waylon Bailey. *Micah, Nahum, Habakkuk, and Zephaniah*. NAC. Nashville: Broadman & Holman, 1997.

Well done exposition that would benefit any pastor.

Feinberg, Charles Lee. *Micah: Wrath Upon Samaria and Jerusalem*. New York: American Board of Missions to the Jews, 1951.

See under "The Minor Prophets" above.

Kaiser, Walter. *Micah-Malachi*. TPC. Nashville: Thomas Nelson, 1992.

Helpful outlines and illustrations for preaching in this volume.

McComiskey, Thomas. *Micah*. REBC 8. Revised. Grand Rapids: Zondervan, 2008.

See under McComiskey in "Minor Prophets" above.

Smith, Gary. *Hosea, Amos, Micah*. NIVAC. Grand Rapids: Zondervan, 2001.

See above under Hosea.

Waltke, Bruce. "Micah." *The Minor Prophets*. Vol. 2. Thomas McComiskey, ed. Grand Rapids: Baker, 2009.

See under McComiskey in "Minor Prophets" above.

_____. *A Commentary on Micah*. Grand Rapids: Eerdmans, 2007.

This is simply one of the finest commentaries by a brilliant Old Testament scholar. Longman calls it the most comprehensive and insightful on Micah today. It is marred somewhat by his Reformed perspective of replacement theology with respect to Israel.

## SERMONS

Calvin, John. *Sermons on the Book of Micah*. Trans. and ed. by Benjamin Farley. Phillipsburg, NJ: P&R, 2003.

Calvin's sermons are always worth a look. Here are 28 on Micah.

# NAHUM

## EXEGETICAL COMMENTARIES

Maier, Walter. *The Book of Nahum: A Commentary*. St. Louis: Concordia, 1959. [Minneapolis: James Family, 1977 reprint].

Excellent volume by the famous radio Bible teacher of the "Lutheran Hour" and Professor of Hebrew and Old Testament at Concordia Seminary whose Ph.D. was in Semitics from Harvard. He died in 1950. His personal interest was Nahum, and he carried on an extensive exegetical study over a period of years, the fruit of which can be found here. Evangelical to the bone. If you are preaching on Nahum, don't neglect this volume.

Patterson, Richard. *Nahum, Habakkuk, Zephaniah*. WEC. Chicago: Moody, 1991.

Outstanding conservative, detailed work backed by scholarly awareness and expertise, according to Rosscup.

## EXPOSITORY COMMENTARIES

Baker, David. *Nahum, Habakkuk, Zephaniah*. TOTC. Downers Grove: InterVarsity, 2008.

Brief but helpful exposition for preachers.

Barker, Ken and Waylon Bailey. *Micah, Nahum, Habakkuk, and Zephaniah*. NAC. Nashville: Broadman & Holman, 1997.

See above under Micah.

Bruckner, James. *Jonah, Nahum, Habakkuk, Zephaniah*. NIVAC. Grand Rapids: Zondervan, 2004.

Preachers will find solid, basic exposition but good application in this volume.

Longman, Tremper. "Nahum." *The Minor Prophets*. Vol. 2. T. McComiskey, ed. Grand Rapids: Baker, 2009.

See under McComiskey in "Minor Prophets" above.

Robertson, O. P. *The Books of Nahum, Habakkuk, and Zephaniah*. NICOT. Grand Rapids: Eerdmans, 1990.

Longman considers it strong on theological analysis and application.

# HABAKKUK

## EXEGETICAL COMMENTARIES

Andersen, Francis I. *Habakkuk*. AYBC. New Haven: Yale University Press, 2001.

Glynn calls it "exhaustive."

Patterson, Richard. *Nahum, Habakkuk, Zephaniah*. WEC. Chicago: Moody, 1991 [republished by Biblical Studies in 2003.]

See under Nahum.

## EXPOSITORY COMMENTARIES

Baker, David. *Nahum, Habakkuk, Zephaniah*. TOTC. Downers Grove: InterVarsity, 2008.

See under Nahum above.

Barker, Ken and Waylon Bailey. *Micah, Nahum, Habakkuk, and Zephaniah*. NAC. Nashville: Broadman & Holman, 1997.

See under Micah above.

Bruce, F. F. "Habakkuk." *The Minor Prophets*, Ed. by T. McComiskey. Grand Rapids: Baker, 2009.

See under McComiskey in "Minor Prophets" above.

Bruckner, James. *Jonah, Nahum, Habakkuk, Zephaniah*. NIVAC. Grand Rapids: Zondervan, 2004.

See under Jonah above.

Feinberg, Charles Lee. *Habakkuk: Problems of Faith*. New York: American Board of Missions to the Jews, 1951.

See above under "The Minor Prophets."

Kaiser, Walter. *Micah-Malachi*. TPC. Nashville: Thomas Nelson, 1992.

See under Micah above.

Robertson, O. P. *The Books of Nahum, Habakkuk, and Zephaniah*. NICOT. Grand Rapids: Eerdmans, 1990.

See above under Nahum.

## SERMONS

Lloyd-Jones, David Martyn. *From Fear to Faith*. London: InterVarsity, 1953.

Expository messages on Habakkuk from the famed pastor of London's Westminster Chapel.

# ZEPHANIAH

## EXEGETICAL COMMENTARIES

Patterson, Richard. *Nahum, Habakkuk, Zephaniah*. WEC. Chicago: Moody, 1991.

> Probably the most helpful exegetical commentary that is conservative in nature.

## EXPOSITORY COMMENTARIES

Baker, David. *Nahum, Habakkuk, Zephaniah*. TOTC. Downers Grove: InterVarsity, 2008.

> See under Nahum above.

Barker, Ken and Waylon Bailey. *Micah, Nahum, Habakkuk, and Zephaniah*. NAC. Nashville: Broadman & Holman, 1997.

> See under Micah above.

Bruckner, James. *Jonah, Nahum, Habakkuk, Zephaniah*. NIVAC. Grand Rapids: Zondervan, 2004.

> See under Jonah above.

Feinberg, Charles. *Zephaniah: The Day of the Lord*. New York: American Board of Missions to the Jews, 1951.

> See under "The Minor Prophets" above.

Kaiser, Walter. *Micah-Malachi*. TPC. Nashville: Thomas Nelson, 1992.

> See under Micah above.

Kleinert, Paul. *The Book of Zephaniah*. Charles Elliott, trans. Grand Rapids: Zondervan, 1960.

> A superb work. Well-researched, readable, complete, and helpful homiletically, says Moo.

Motyer, J. A. "Zephaniah." *The Minor Prophets*. Vol. 3. T. McComiskey, ed. Grand Rapids: Baker, 2008.

> See under McComiskey in "Minor Prophets" above.

Robertson, O. P. *The Books of Nahum, Habakkuk, and Zephaniah*. NICOT. Grand Rapids: Eerdmans, 1990.

> See under Nahum above.

Walker, Larry L. *Zephaniah*. REBC 8. Grand Rapids: Zondervan, 2009.

Good exposition on Zephaniah from a recognized Old Testament Scholar. Helpful for pastors.

Webber, Daniel. *The Coming of the Warrior-King: Zephaniah Simply Explained*. WCS. Darlington: Evangelical Press, 2004.

Brief but good exposition and application written with the preacher in mind.

## DEVOTIONAL COMMENTARIES

Allen, Ronald. *A Shelter in the Fury: A Prophet's Stunning Picture of God*. Portland, OR: Multnomah, 1986.

Preachers will find homiletical help here.

# HAGGAI

## EXEGETICAL COMMENTARIES

Merrill, Eugene. *Haggai, Zechariah, Malachi: An Exegetical Commentary*. Spokane: Biblical Studies Press, 2003 reprint.

Excellent work form the pen of a respected OT scholar at Dallas Theological Seminary. Readable for the pastor. I would use this volume if preaching through these books.

## EXPOSITORY COMMENTARIES

Boda, Mark J. *Haggai, Zechariah*. NIVAC. Grand Rapids: Zondervan, 2004.

Academic & pastoral. Longman gives it 5 stars.

Hill, Andrew. *Haggai, Zechariah and Malachi: An Introduction and Commentary*. TOTC. Downers Grove: Intervarsity, 2012.

Brief, concise, and helpful exposition for the pastor from the reputable TOTC series.

Feinberg, Charles Lee. *Haggai: Rebuilding the Temple*. New York: American Board of Missions to the Jews, 1951.

See under "The Minor Prophets" above.

Kaiser, Walter. *Micah-Malachi*. TPC. Nashville: Thomas Nelson, 1992.

See above on Micah.

Merrill, Eugene H. *Haggai*. REBC 8. Grand Rapids: Zondervan, 2009.

See under Merrill above.

Motyer, J. A. "Haggai." *The Minor Prophets*, Vol. 3. T. McComiskey, ed. Grand Rapids: Baker, 2009.

See above under McComiskey in "Minor Prophets"

Taylor, Richard A. and E. Ray Clendenen. *Haggai and Malachi*. NAC. Nashville: Broadman & Holman, 2004.

Taylor treats Haggai and Clendenen covers Malachi. Both are solid works. Clendenen employs aspects of discourse analysis to aid in the interpretation of Malachi.

Verhoef, Pieter A. *The Books of Haggai and Malachi*. NICOT. Grand Rapids: Eerdmans, 1987.

Verhoef was a conservative Old Testament professor at the University of Stellenbosch, South Africa.

Wolf, Herbert. *Haggai and Malachi*. Chicago: Moody, 1976.

Pastors will benefit here.

# ZECHARIAH

## EXEGETICAL COMMENTARIES

Merrill, Eugene. *Haggai, Zechariah, Malachi: An Exegetical Commentary*. Spokane: Biblical Studies Press, 2003.

See above under Haggai.

## EXPOSITORY COMMENTARIES

Barker, Kenneth L. *Zechariah*. REBC 8. Revised. Grand Rapids: Zondervan, 2008.

Very fine treatment. Premillennial.

Baron, David. *The Visions and Prophecies of Zechariah*. 3rd ed. London: Morgan & Scott, 1919.

Expositional and devotional study by a Jewish Christian scholar who brings to bear his knowledge of rabbinic sources to the text. Kaiser called it a "rich treat of theology and exegesis." Wilbur Smith said this volume should be in every Bible student's library. Not to be missed! More than 550 pages.

Boda, Mark J. *Haggai, Zechariah*. NIVAC. Grand Rapids: Zondervan, 2004.

Good exposition and application designed for the expository preacher.

Feinberg, Charles Lee. *God Remembers: A Study of the Book of Zechariah*. New York: American Board of Missions to the Jews, 1965 [4th ed. published by Multnomah in 1979.]

See under "The Minor Prophets" above. Excellent volume with Scripture index and helpful selected annotated bibliography. Feinberg taught Zechariah for many years in Hebrew exegetical courses at Dallas Theological Seminary and Talbot Seminary.

Hill, Andrew. *Haggai, Zechariah and Malachi: An Introduction and Commentary*. TOTC. Downers Grove: Intervarsity, 2012.

Brief, concise, and helpful exposition for the pastor from the reputable TOTC series.

Kaiser, Walter. *Micah-Malachi*. TPC. Nashville: Thomas Nelson, 1992.

See above under Micah.

Klein, George. *Zechariah*. NAC. Nashville: Broadman & Holman, 2007.

Excellent volume from the pen of the Senior Associate Dean for PhD Studies at Southwestern Baptist Theological Seminary. Thoughtful exegesis from a Premillennial standpoint.

Leupold, H. C. *Zechariah*. Grand Rapids: Baker, 1971.

A very helpful volume for the expositor by a pastor/scholar in the evangelical Lutheran tradition. Amillennial perspective. Moo says it is outstanding, complete, well-researched, and evangelical.

McComiskey, Thomas. "Zechariah." *The Minor Prophets*. Vol. 3. T. McComiskey, ed. Grand Rapids: Baker, 2008.

See under McComiskey in "Minor Prophets" above.

Unger, Merrill. *Zechariah: Prophet of Messiah's Glory*. Grand Rapids: Zondervan, 1963.

Excellent exposition based on the Hebrew text. The result of more than 15 years of lectures on Zechariah at Dallas Theological Seminary – Rosscup.

Webb, Barry G. *The Message of Zechariah: Your Kingdom Come*. BST. Downers Grove: InterVarsity, 2003.

Webb is head of Old Testament Studies at Moore Theological College in Australia. This is a solid exposition.

Wright, Charles H. H. *Zechariah and His Prophecies*. Bampton Lectures, 1878. London: Hodder & Stoughton, 1879 [also reprinted and published by Klock & Klock, 1980].

Feinberg considers this "A masterpiece on the prophecy of Zechariah. ... Especially useful is the critical and grammatical commentary at the end of the volume. No one can claim to be well-read on the prophecy of Zechariah who has not pondered this tome." Almost 700 pages but worth your time! Amillennial perspective.

## DEVOTIONAL COMMENTARIES

Meyer, F. B. *The Prophet of Hope: Studies in Zechariah*. New York: Revell, 1900.

From the pen of a Baptist pastor in London and contemporary of Spurgeon. Meyer cannot be one-upped when it comes to devotional treatment of anything!

# MALACHI

## EXEGETICAL COMMENTARIES

Hill, Andrew. *Malachi*. AB. New Haven: Yale University Press, 2008.

> Extensive analysis of introductory matters and good exposition. Considers the books connection with the New Testament as well.

Merrill, Eugene. *Haggai, Zechariah, Malachi: An Exegetical Commentary*. Spokane: Biblical Studies Press, 2003 reprint.

> See under Haggai.

## EXPOSITORY COMMENTARIES

Adam, Peter. *The Message of Malachi: I Have Loved You, Says the Lord*. BST. Downers Grove: IVP Academic, 2013.

> Helpful treatment from the author of an excellent work on the theology of preaching entitled *Preaching God's Words*."

Baker, David W. *Joel, Obadiah, Malachi*. NIVAC. Grand Rapids: Zondervan, 2006.

> See above under Joel.

Benton, John. *Losing Touch with the Living God: Malachi Simply Explained*. WCS. Darlington: Evangelical, 1985.

> The title says it all.

Blaising, Craig. "Malachi." BKC. Vol. 1. Wheaton: Victor, 1983.

> One of the earliest works by the distinguished scholar/theologian who leads the charge for Progressive Dispensationalism. Pastors will find solid exposition here.

Feinberg, Charles Lee. *Malachi: Formal Worship*. New York: American Board of Missions to the Jews, 1951.

> See under "The Minor Prophets" above.

Hill, Andrew. *Haggai, Zechariah and Malachi: An Introduction and Commentary*. TOTC. Downers Grove: Intervarsity, 2012.

> See under Haggai above.

Kaiser, Walter. *Micah-Malachi*. TPC. Nashville: Thomas Nelson, 1992.

> Fine treatment by a well-recognized Old Testament scholar who taught Old Testament and served as dean and vice president at Trinity Evangelical.

_____. *Malachi: God's Unchanging Love*. Grand Rapids: Baker, 1984.

> See above. Barber says of it: "a work of exceptional merit. Demonstrates the goal of true exposition: the synthesis of scholarship with devotion so that the text of Scripture is clearly and adequately explained ... Highly recommended."

Merrill, Eugene H. *Malachi*. REBC 8. Grand Rapids: Zondervan, 2009.

> Clear, concise and helpful treatment of Malachi from a well-recognized Professor of Old Testament at Dallas Theological Seminary.

Morgan, G. Campbell. *Malachi's Message for Today*. Grand Rapids: Baker, 1972.

> Vintage Morgan. Consult when preaching through Malachi.

Stuart, Douglas. "Malachi." *The Minor Prophets*, Ed. by Thomas McComiskey. Grand Rapids: Baker, 2009.

> See under "McComiskey" in "Minor Prophets" above.

Taylor, Richard A. and E. Ray Clendenen. *Haggai and Malachi*. NAC. Nashville: Broadman & Holman, 2004.

> Clendenen's treatment of Malachi is the fruit of years of study and has a linguistic focus that aids in understanding the text.

Verhoef, Pieter A. *The Books of Haggai and Malachi*. NICOT. Grand Rapids: Eerdmans, 1987.

> See above under Haggai.

# *The*
# NEW
# TESTAMENT

# MATTHEW

## EXEGETICAL COMMENTARIES

Davies, W.D. and Dale Allison. *Matthew*. 3 vols. ICC. Edinburgh: T. & T. Clark, 1988, 1991, 1997.

Top of the line exegetical work that is very detailed. Not for the faint-hearted. One might consult the one volume abridged edition—*Matthew: A Shorter Commentary* (London; New York: T. & T. Clark International, 2004)

Nolland, John. *The Gospel of Matthew*. NIGTC. Grand Rapids: Eerdmans, 2005.

Helpful on exegesis, but watch for some pitfalls, including his denial of Matthean authorship and use of redaction and narrative criticism along the way.

Osborne, Grant R. *Matthew*. ZECNT. Grand Rapids: Zondervan, 2010.

Osborne always delivers. Strong on exegesis of the Greek text.

Plummer, Alfred. *An Exegetical Commentary on the Gospel According to St. Matthew*. Grand Rapids: Baker, 1982.

First published in 1915, Barber says it "remains one of the best treatments of Matthew's Gospel ever written."

Turner, David L. *Matthew*. BECNT. Grand Rapids: Baker, 2008.

A solid exegetical work. Premillennial perspective. The Baker Exegetical series is turning out excellent volumes that are meaty and lengthy.

## EXPOSITIONAL COMMENTARIES

Blomberg, Craig L. *Matthew*. NAC. Nashville: Broadman & Holman, 2001.

Blomberg is always thorough and conservative. Premillennial perspective.

Broadus, John Albert. *Commentary on the Gospel of Matthew*. Grand Rapids: Kregel, 1990.

From the old American Commentary series [Baptist], this is the only volume in that series that is worth using today. Broadus was one of the founders of Southern Baptist Theological Seminary and wrote a classic work on preaching that should be in every preacher's library. His Matthew volume abounds in helpful material for the preacher. His knowledge of patristic and medieval work on Matthew is evident in his many quotations from these sources. This commentary remains a solid resource for interpreting and preaching Matthew.

Carson, D. A. *Matthew*. REBC 9. Grand Rapids: Zondervan, 2010.

Carson is always reliable and gets to the point of the text.

France, R. T. *The Gospel of Matthew*. NICNT. Grand Rapids: Eerdmans, 2007.

Excellent and massive work (over 1,200 pages); the result of a lifetime of research on Matthew, but watch out for some of his interpretations, especially his eschatological approach.

Keener, Craig S. *The Gospel of Matthew: A Socio-Rhetorical Commentary*. Grand Rapids: Eerdmans, 1999.

While I'm not as sold on the new wave of socio-rhetorical commentaries as some are (though they do contain helpful information), this volume will prove to be helpful to the preacher, particularly in the area of application.

Wilkins, Michael J. *Matthew*. NIVAC. Grand Rapids: Zondervan, 2004.

True to the series' aim, Wilkins delivers basic exposition followed by helpful application ideas for the preacher.

## DEVOTIONAL COMMENTARIES

Morison, James. *A Practical Commentary on the Gospel According to St. Matthew*. Minneapolis: Klock & Klock, 1981 reprint.

This Scottish expository preacher has a heart for God! "The practical and devotional thoughts alone are worth many times the cost of the book," says Barber.

Morrison, George H. *Morrison on Matthew*. 3 vols. Glasgow Pulpit Series. Chattanooga, TN: AMG, 1978.

The Scottish Morrison spent 15 months under the tutelage of the great Alexander Whyte. His final pastorate was Wellington Church, Glasgow, from 1902 until his death in 1928. Though he does not cover all of Matthew, what he does cover is definitely worth reading! I have tried to collect all of his books of sermons. Brilliant wordsmith.

Spurgeon, Charles. *The Gospel of the Kingdom: A Commentary on the Book of Matthew*. Grand Rapids: Zondervan, 1964.

First published in 1893—a year after Spurgeon's death—this is a helpful volume for practical application in preaching.

## STUDIES ON THE SERMON ON THE MOUNT

Boice, James M. *The Sermon on the Mount*. Grand Rapids: Baker, 2002.

Very helpful sermons from one of my favorite Presbyterian pastors.

Chappell, Clovis Gillham. *Sermon on the Mount*. New York: Abingdon, 1930.

Chappell was a Methodist pastor famous for his many books of sermons, especially his sermons on Bible characters. This series of sermons will be helpful to any pastor.

Guelich, Robert A. *The Sermon on the Mount: A Foundation for Understanding*. Waco, TX: Word, 1982.

An excellent 450-page treatment that should not be overlooked when preaching on the Sermon on the Mount.

Hughes, R. Kent. *The Sermon on the Mount*. Wheaton: Crossway, 2001.

Very helpful volume by a noted expository preacher for many years at The College Church in Wheaton, Ill., and editor of the *Preaching the Word* series published by Crossway. Don't miss Hughes' illustrations.

Lloyd-Jones, David Martyn. *Studies in the Sermon on the Mount*. Grand Rapids: Eerdmans, 1984.

You cannot afford to be without this volume if you plan to preach on the Sermon! Marvelous expositional studies with practical application by the master Welsh pastor/expositor of The Westminster Chapel in London from 1943 until 1968.

Pink, Arthur. *An Exposition of the Sermon on the Mount*. Grand Rapids: Baker, 1950.

I'm not as sold on Pink as some are since he goes to extremes with his Reformed theology and his typology. However, this work is a good expository treatment of the Sermon that also contains much practical application. I've used it many times.

Quarles, Charles L. *Sermon on the Mount: Restoring Christ's Message in the Modern Church*. NACSBT. Nashville: Broadman & Holman, 2011.

One of the best newer works on the Sermon on the Mount. Very helpful to pastors.

Robinson, Haddon. *The Christian Salt and Light Company: A Contemporary Study of the Sermon on the Mount*. Grand Rapids: Discovery House Publishing, 1988; and *The Solid Rock Construction Company*. Grand Rapids: Discovery House Publishing, 1989.

Helpful two volumes for preachers by the dean of evangelical homileticians. *Salt and Light Company* covers Matthew 5; *Solid Rock* covers Matthew 6–7. Lots of good preaching ideas.

Stott, John. *Christian Counter-Culture: The Message of the Sermon on the Mount*. Downers Grove: InterVarsity, 1978.

If Stott writes on it, the preacher should consult it!

## STUDIES ON THE BEATITUDES

Boreham, Frank. *The Heavenly Octave*. New York: Abir. ;don, 1936.

According to Barber, these messages are "colorful and ( loquent." Boreham was a master wordsmith and author of more than 50 books. Highly recommended to preachers for its homiletical value. Boreham was a favorite author of John Phillips, many of whose illustrations in his own commentaries come from Boreham. Boreham is also a favorite of Ravi Zacharias, whose ministry blog "A Slice of Infinity" takes its title from one of Boreham's essays.

Maclaren, Alexander. *A Garland of Gladness*. Grand Rapids: Eerdmans, 1945.

These devotional messages were originally published in the late 19th century. Maclaren was such a superb expositor whose work I always try to read.

Wiersbe, Warren. *Live Like a King: Making the Beatitudes Work in Daily Life*. Chicago: Moody, 1976.

I own everything Wiersbe wrote and always consult him if possible before preaching. His strength is illustration and practical application. Barber calls it "a devotional masterpiece."

# MARK

## EXEGETICAL COMMENTARIES

France, R. T. *The Gospel of Mark*. NIGTC. Grand Rapids: Eerdmans, 2002.

Over 700 pages. More historical/theological than exegetical. Deals with text by sections rather than verse by verse, says Glynn. Careful and detailed, says Bauer.

Stein, Robert H. *Mark*. BECNT. Grand Rapids: Baker, 2008.

Solid exegesis, conservative. See below on Luke.

## EXPOSITORY COMMENTARIES

Edwards, James R. *The Gospel According to Mark*. PNTC. Grand Rapids: Eerdmans, 2001.

The Pillar series of commentaries runs very strong on solid exposition of the text. This volume is no exception.

Garland, David E. *Mark*. NIVAC. Grand Rapids: Zondervan, 1996.

I have found Garland to be a thorough, well-balanced commentator. If he writes on it, I try to read him. True to the NIVAC series' intent, this volume is a good balance between exposition and application.

Hiebert, D. Edmond. *The Gospel of Mark: An Expositional Commentary*. Greenville, SC: Bob Jones University Press, 1994.

I have consulted Hiebert's books for years. Great help to the expositor. Hiebert has a knack for getting at the heart of meaning.

Lane, William L. *The Gospel of Mark*. NICNT. Grand Rapids: Eerdmans, 1974.

Lane was a Baptist scholar. This volume employs some redaction criticism but addresses the literary structure of the book well. Attention to theological reflection on the text, says Bauer. Lane is probably best known for his two-volume work on Hebrews in the WBC series.

Swete, Henry Barclay. *The Gospel According to St. Mark*. Grand Rapids: Eerdmans, 1978 reprint [1898].

First rate scholarship from this Cambridge scholar, but Carson calls it "dull and stodgy." Still helpful though for the preacher in my judgment. Amillennial perspective.

Morrison, George H. *Morrison on Mark*. Glasgow Pulpit Series. Ridgefield, N.J.: AMG, 1977.

See above under Matthew.

Morison, James. *A Practical Commentary on the Gospel According to St. Mark*. 4th revised ed. Minneapolis: Klock & Klock, 1981 reprint.

See above on Matthew. Strength of exposition far outweighs its syntactical deficiencies, says Barber.

# LUKE

## EXEGETICAL COMMENTARIES

Bock, Darrell L. *Luke*. 2 vols. BECNT. Grand Rapids: Baker, 1994, 1996.

> Best exegetical commentary on Luke to date by a well-known New Testament professor and prolific author at Dallas Theological Seminary. A must for those preaching through Luke.

Garland, David E. *Luke*. ZECNT. Grand Rapids: Zondervan, 2011.

> Over 1,000 pages of solid exegetical and expositional help from the pen of one of the finest evangelical commentators.

Marshall, I. Howard. *The Gospel of Luke*. NIGTC. Grand Rapids: Eerdmans, 1978.

> Before Bock, this would probably have been my top choice for Luke in the exegetical category. Marshall is a balanced and well-respected New Testament scholar. Watch for some issues with redaction criticism. Assumes Luke is drawing from Mark and Q.

## EXPOSITORY COMMENTARIES

Godet, F. *A Commentary on the Gospel of St. Luke*. Eugene, OR: Wipf & Stock, 2004 reprint.

> I usually try to read any commentary this conservative French scholar of yesteryear wrote. Though pre-critical, the preacher will find good help here. Godet incorporates some warm devotional thoughts along the way in his works.

Green, Joel B. *The Gospel of Luke*. NICNT. Grand Rapids: Eerdmans, 1997.

> Just shy of 1,000 pages, this is one of the serious works on Luke. Green focuses well on aspects of discourse analysis that aid in understanding Luke's overall structure at the micro and macro level. Use as a supplement to Stein or one of the other expository commentaries.

Hendriksen, William. *Exposition of the Gospel According to Luke*. Grand Rapids: Baker, 1978.

> Probably the best from the pen of this professor of New Testament literature at Calvin Seminary.

Stein, Robert H. *Luke*. NAC. Nashville: Broadman & Holman, 1993.

Stein's work is always solid and evangelical. This is one of the best expository commentaries on Luke.

## DEVOTIONAL COMMENTARIES

Morgan, G. Campbell. *The Gospel According to Luke*. New York: Revell, 1931.

"A carefully reasoned exposition which adheres quite closely to Luke's argument and provides an example of expository preaching at its best," says Barber. Premillennial, but Morgan abandoned premillennialism later in life.

Morrison, George H. *Morrison on Luke*. 2 vols. Glasgow Pulpit Series. Chattanooga, TN: AMG, 1978.

See under Matthew.

## SPECIAL STUDIES

Bock, Darrell L. *A Theology of Luke and Acts*. Grand Rapids: Zondervan, 2012.

See on Bock above.

Liddon, H. P. *The Magnificat*. 3rd ed. London: Longman's Green & Co., 1898.

These sermons were preached in St. Paul's Cathedral by one of England's well-known evangelical preachers.

# JOHN

## EXEGETICAL COMMENTARIES

Barrett, C. K. *The Gospel According to St. John: An Introduction with Commentary and Notes on the Greek Text*. Revised. London: SPCK, 1988.

> Barrett is a mixed bag. He is none too concerned with historical issues but sees the book as a theological unity. His work remains one of the top commentaries on John.

Keener, Craig S. *The Gospel of John*. 2 vols. Peabody, MA: Hendrickson, 2003.

> A massive tome of 1,636 pages! No stone left unturned here!

Köstenberger, Andreas J. *John*. BECNT. Grand Rapids: Baker, 2004.

> A well-written commentary from the professor of New Testament at Southeastern Baptist Seminary. John is Köstenberger's specialty. Consult it.

Westcott, B. F. *The Gospel According to St. John*. Grand Rapids: Eerdmans, 1950.

> Originally published in 1881, this work is still a masterpiece of exegesis. He was called "in learning a second Origen; in piety a second Augustine." G. Campbell Morgan said of it: "... not a finer has been written on the Gospel of John than Westcott's commentary."

## EXPOSITORY COMMENTARIES

Borchert, Gerald L. *John 1–11*. NAC. Nashville: Broadman & Holman, 1996.

> A worthy exposition of John. Solid and helpful for the expository preacher.

_____. *John 12–21*. NAC. Nashville: Broadman & Holman, 2002.

> See above.

Burge, Gary M. *John*. NIVAC. Grand Rapids: Zondervan, 2000.

> I like what Burge has done with 1 John, and this work on John is also very helpful.

Carson, D. A. *The Gospel According to John*. PNTC. Grand Rapids: Eerdmans, 1990.

See under Matthew above. One will find solid exegesis and exposition designed especially for the preacher.

Godet, F. *Commentary on John's Gospel*. Grand Rapids: Kregel, 1980 reprint. 2 vols in one.

See on Luke above. This volume was first published in English in 1893. Barber says, "Thorough and exhaustive without being elaborate or verbose. ... One of the finest expositions of John's gospel ever produced. No preacher should be without it." Smith said of it: "Here are some of the finest pages of Christology to be found anywhere."

Michaels, J. Ramsey. *The Gospel of John*. NICNT. Grand Rapids: Eerdmans, 2010.

Thankfully uninterested in source and redaction criticism, Michaels deals with the text we have. Detailed, verse by verse, deals with the Greek but is accessible to pastors. Attempts to see the cohesive whole of John's Gospel. This is the fruit of Michaels' lifetime work on John.

Morris, Leon. *The Gospel According to John*. NICNT. Revised ed. Grand Rapids: Eerdmans, 1995.

Assumes historical reliability of John as well as the theological nature of the book. Contains a "subtle richness and depth," says Bauer. Barber says, "Superlative scholarship." No preacher can afford to be without this commentary when preaching on John.

## DEVOTIONAL COMMENTARIES

Mitchell, John G. *An Everlasting Love: A Devotional Study of the Gospel of John*. Portland, OR: Multnomah, 1982.

Excellent devotional commentary from the pen of the founder of Multnomah School of the Bible and pastor of Central Bible Church in Portland. Don't miss the illustrations and applications.

Van Doren, William. *Gospel of John*. 2 volumes in one. Grand Rapids: Kregel, 1981.

Lots of sermonic help here from this hefty volume!

## SPECIAL STUDIES

Bernard, Thomas Dehany. *The Central Teaching of Christ: A Study of John 13–17*. Minneapolis: Klock & Klock, 1985 reprint [1892].

"A must for every pastor," says Barber.

Blomberg, Craig. *The Historical Reliability of John's Gospel: Issues & Commentary*. Downers Grove: InterVarsity, 2011.

Glynn describes it as 223 pages of commentary, 50 pages of introduction, and a useful 32-page bibliography.

Brown, John. *Exposition of Our Lord's Intercessory Prayer*. Minneapolis: Klock & Klock, 1978.

Brown was both pastor and exegete. This work is worth consulting. "His exposition serves as a model," says Barber.

Köstenberger, Andreas J. and Scott R. Swain. *Father, Son, and Spirit: The Trinity and John's Gospel*. Downers Grove: InterVarsity, 2008.

The title says it all. Helpful volume.

Maclaren, Alexander. *The Holy of Holies*. London: Alexander & Shepheard, 1890.

Very good expository sermons on John 14–16 by the master Baptist expositor and contemporary of Spurgeon.

Rainsford, Marcus. *Our Lord Prays for His Own*. Grand Rapids: Kregel, 1985 [1895].

Regarded by many as the greatest classic ever written on John 17. Rainsford pastored St. John's Church in London from 1886 to his death in 1897. Barber calls it a true masterpiece of devotional and expositional literature. This volume is a must.

Swete, Henry Barclay. *The Last Discourse and Prayer of Our Lord*. London: Macmillan, 1914.

## SERMONS

Lloyd-Jones, David Martyn. *John 17*. 4 volumes. Wheaton: Crossway, 1988–89.

Expositions from sermons preached in 1952–53 at Westminster Chapel. Moving devotional material here.

# ACTS

## EXEGETICAL COMMENTARIES

Barrett, C. K. *Acts*. 2 vols. ICC. Edinburgh: T. & T. Clark, 1994, 1998.

> Barrett's magnum opus reflects decades of study on Acts. Chock full of exegetical and theological data.

Bock, Darrell L. *Acts*. BECNT. Grand Rapids: Baker, 2007.

> Counterpart to his Luke commentary. Not one to be missed!

Gloag, Paton J. *A Critical and Exegetical Commentary on the Acts of the Apostles*. 2 vols. Minneapolis: Klock & Klock, 1979 [1870].

> Gloag was a Scottish Presbyterian. Barber: "A thorough exposition based on careful exegesis." Spurgeon quotes Hackett: "It shows a thorough mastery of the material, philology, history, and literature pertaining to this range of study, and a skill in the use of this knowledge, which places it in the first class of modern expositions."

Keener, Craig S. *Acts: An Exegetical Commentary, Vol. 1: Introduction and 1:1–2:47*. Grand Rapids: Baker, 2012.

> At more than 1,000 pages, there is no telling how long the projected four-volume work will be! The second volume, *Acts: An Exegetical Commentary, Vol. 2: 3:1-14:28* released in late 2013. Top-notch material. Must be reckoned among the top five commentaries on Acts.

Schnabel, Eckhard. *Acts*. ZECNT. Grand Rapids: Zondervan, 2012.

> Schnabel's *Acts* is a thorough analysis of the book. It must now be considered one of the best commentaries on the book. Very up to date on all issues. Expository preachers will want to make use of this volume.

## EXPOSITORY COMMENTARIES

Bruce, F. F. *The Book of Acts*. NICNT. Grand Rapids: Eerdmans, 1988.

> This work is still helpful to pastors preaching on Acts. See also his *The Acts of the Apostles: The Greek Text with Introduction and Commentary*. 3rd ed. Revised and enlarged. Grand Rapids: Eerdmans, 1990. This work would be helpful to pastors with knowledge of Greek. Bauer said Bruce was "a classicist by training and a historian by temperament." Both are evident in this conservative commentary.

Fernando, Ajith. *Acts*. NIVAC. Grand Rapids: Zondervan, 1998.

> Majors on exposition and application, with illustrations for use in preaching.

Harrison, Everett. *Interpreting Acts: The Expanding Church*. Grand Rapids: Zondervan, 1986.

Expository preachers will find lots of good help here. Though the discussion of each section is brief, it is on target.

Larkin, William. *Acts*. IVPNTC. Downers Grove: InterVarsity, 1995.

Very good work from the long time Professor of New Testament and Greek at Columbia Biblical Seminary and Graduate School of Missions in Columbia, SC. Larkin passed away earlier in 2014. I have always benefited from anything Larkin wrote.

Marshall, I. Howard. *The Acts of the Apostles*. TNTC. Grand Rapids: Eerdmans, 2007.

Solid, readable, and concise material, just as we've come to expect from Marshall.

Peterson, David G. *The Acts of the Apostles*. PNTC. Grand Rapids: Eerdmans, 2009.

Peterson's *Acts* is a worthy addition to the Pillar series. He has done considerable work on the book. Preachers will find this a strong expository treatment that touches virtually all the bases.

Polhill, John B. *Acts*. NAC. Nashville: Broadman & Holman, 1992.

A solid help to expository preachers by a Baptist scholar. Amillennial perspective. See more detailed annotation in Rosscup.

Rackham, R. B. *The Acts of the Apostles*. Grand Rapids: Baker, 1978 [1901].

Carson says, "Rackham was a devout high churchman, shrewd in his practical comments." Barber calls it one of the greatest commentaries on Acts and says it deserves to be regarded as a classic. I used it when I preached through Acts and found it helpful. Conservative and amillennial.

Stott, John. *The Message of Acts: The Spirit, the Church & the World*. BST. Downers Grove: InterVarsity, 1994.

Anything by John Stott is worth consulting. Always clear, succinct, and helpful.

Walker, Thomas. *The Acts of the Apostles*. Chicago: Moody, 1965.

This work was originally published in 1910 and written for missionaries. Smith says of it: "without question the greatest commentary on the book of Acts from a missionary standpoint."

## DEVOTIONAL COMMENTARIES

Alexander, Joseph. *Commentary on the Acts of the Apostles*. 2 vols. in one. Grand Rapids: Zondervan, 1956/Minneapolis: Klock & Klock, 1980 reprint.

Originally published in 19th century. One of the best of the devotional commentaries on Acts. Barber calls it "an exhaustive, thorough exposition … [that] provides preachers with an abundance of usable material." Reformed perspective.

Griffith Thomas, W. H. *Outline Studies in the Acts of the Apostles*. Grand Rapids: Eerdmans,1956.

The strength of this work is its detailed outlines.

Morgan, G. Campbell. *The Acts of the Apostles*. New York: Revell, 1924.

Very helpful exposition and application for the pastor. Smith called it the greatest expository volume given us by any English or American expository preacher—a monumental work, profound and practical.

Ogilvie, Lloyd John. *Acts*. CC. Waco, TX: Word, 1983.

Ogilvie was the editor of the Communicator's Commentary, and this is one of the best commentaries in this series. He was a seasoned pastor and expositor. For sermons on Acts, see his *The Drumbeat of Love* [1976].

## SPECIAL STUDIES

Bock, Darrell L. *A Theology of Luke and Acts: God's Promised Program, Realized for All Nations*. Grand Rapids: Zondervan, 2012.

This work and that by Marshall and Peterson below are the two best studies on the theology of Luke and Acts.

Marshall, I. Howard and David Peterson, eds. *Witness to the Gospel: The Theology of Acts*. Grand Rapids: Eerdmans, 1998.

This work along with Bock's above are the two best studies on the theology of Acts. Contains 25 essays written by prominent scholars in the field of Lukan studies.

## SERMONS

Vaughan, C. J. *Studies in the Book of Acts*. Minneapolis: Klock & Klock, 1985 reprint.

These "studies" are basically sermons. Vaughan also wrote good expository commentaries on Romans, Philippians, and Revelation. Spurgeon liked this volume. Barber calls it "a work of rare merit."

# ROMANS

## EXEGETICAL COMMENTARIES

Abernathy, C. David. *An Exegetical Summary of Romans 1–8*. 2nd ed. Dallas: SIL International, 2008.

Preachers should own every volume in this excellent series published by the SIL division of Wycliffe Bible Translators. Abernathy surveys 19 commentaries and Greek lexicons and summarizes what they say about lexical, syntactical, and semantic relationships in Romans in a verse-by-verse format. This work is an unbelievable time-saver, though it should not be used in place of commentaries. A semi-literal translation is given, followed by any textual variations, the lexical meanings of key words in context and exegetical questions are presented and then answered in a clear, concise manner. Extremely valuable. I have used them for years.

Cranfield, C. E. B. *Romans*. 2 vols. ICC. Edinburgh: T. & T. Clark, 2004.

Detailed exegesis. Its objectivity is one of its foremost and finest assets, says Martin. Barber calls it a "magisterial handling of the grammar and syntax."

Godet, F. *Commentary on Romans*. Grand Rapids: Kregel, 1977 [1883].

"Exhaustive ... provides an excellent treatment of the argument of the epistle," says Barber.

## EXPOSITORY COMMENTARIES

Barrett, C. K. *Reading Through Romans*. Philadelphia: Fortress Press, 1977.

Martin calls it "a minor masterpiece." You will find it helpful.

Dunn, James D. G. *Romans*. WBC. Dallas: Word, 1988.

A generally good treatment. Excels at tracing both the logic of Paul's argument and the flow of that argument.

Kruse, Colin G. *Paul's Letter to the Romans*. PNTC. Grand Rapids: Eerdmans, 2012.

Intended as the replacement volume for Morris. Kruse bases his almost 600 pages of exegesis in conversation with the scholarly literature, especially of the last 30 years. He writes with clarity and succinctness. He provides a fair assessment of the so-called "New Perspective" of Paul, finding it wanting. Watch for the helpful "additional notes" that expand on theological and interpretive issues along the way. Reformed in orientation. A very important commentary for expository preachers.

Luther, Martin. *Lectures on Romans*. Philadelphia: Westminster, 1961.

Pauck's translation with notes is very helpful to the modern reader. Luther's *Romans* should be in every preacher's library.

McClain, Alva J. *Romans: The Gospel of God's Grace*. Chicago: Moody, 1973.

Many will overlook this volume, but it is worth your time. Premillennial perspective. Very helpful on Romans 9–11.

Moo, Douglas J. *Romans 1–8*. WEC. Chicago: Moody, 1991.

First-rate work by a first-rate New Testament scholar. The exegesis is superb.

_____. *Romans*. NIVAC. Grand Rapids: Zondervan, 2000.

Excellent for preachers. Moo focuses on application, as the series demands. His illustrations are helpful, some from personal experience. His application is timely.

_____. *The Epistle to the Romans*. NICNT. Grand Rapids: Eerdmans, 1996.

As always in this series, the commentary is based on the English text, but Moo's analysis of the Greek is top-notch. Bauer says this work is "fair and balanced."

Morris, Leon. *The Epistle to the Romans*. PNTC. Grand Rapids: Eerdmans, 1988.

Originally published in 1988, this work received the 1989 Gold Medallion for Commentaries from the Evangelical Christian Publishers Association. Slightly Reformed in orientation. At more than 500 pages in length, it is an outstanding work on Romans that no preacher can afford to be without.

Osborne, Grant. *Romans*. IVPNTC. Downers Grove: InterVarsity, 2010.

This is a good exposition of Romans that will be helpful to all preachers. Osborne writes from an Arminian perspective and provides a good balance to Reformed commentaries on Romans.

Robinson, Thomas. *Studies in Romans: Expository and Homiletical*. 2 vols. in one. Grand Rapids: Kregel, 1982 reprint [1878].

875 pages of an amazing combination of scholarship (Greek notes at the end of each verse treatment) coupled with expositional and practical helps galore. Surprising that Carson misses this volume.

Schreiner, Thomas R. *Romans*. BECNT. Grand Rapids: Baker, 1998.

Schreiner, Professor of New Testament at Southern Baptist Theological Seminary, is one of the premier New Testament scholars among Baptists and evangelicals at large. He has provided an excellent treatment of Romans that employs solid exegesis with theological depth. No preacher on Romans should fail to consult Schreiner. Written from a Reformed soteriological perspective.

Stott, John. *The Message of Romans: God's Good News for the World*. Downers Grove: InterVarsity, 1994.

Stott is always conversant with scholarship but excels as an expositor when he treats books of the Bible from his pastoral perspective. This volume is a must-have in my book when preaching through Romans. I recommend you own and read everything by Stott, but lament his annihilationist tendencies.

Vaughan, Curtis and Bruce Corley. *Romans*. SGC. Grand Rapids: Zondervan, 1976.

Excellent, brief but meaty treatment of Romans from Southwestern Seminary's beloved teacher of New Testament and Greek. Vaughan was my favorite professor while a student at Southwestern from 1978–1981, and I now have the privilege of occupying his study carrel containing some of his memorabilia, which he allowed me to keep just before his death. Corley also taught New Testament at Southwestern for many years and wrote his Ph.D. dissertation on Romans 9–11.

## DEVOTIONAL COMMENTARIES

Moule, H. C. G. *The Epistle of St. Paul to the Romans*. EB. Minneapolis: Klock & Klock, 1982.

Devotional exposition very helpful to the preacher. Based upon careful exegesis. Strong on practical application.

Stedman, Ray C. *From Guilt to Glory*. 2 vols. Waco, TX: Word, 1978.

Stedman was a pastor who preached expositionally. This volume's strength is in practical application.

Newell, William R. *Romans: Verse by Verse*. Chicago: Moody, 1948.

One of the finest devotional commentaries on Romans. Not to be missed when preaching through the book. Rosscup noted that Chafer, president of Dallas Theological Seminary until 1952, used to say that Newell knew more about Romans than any man he knew.

## SPECIAL STUDIES

Barnhouse, Donald Grey. *Exposition of Bible Doctrines, Taking the Epistle to the Romans as a Point of Departure*. 10 vols. Grand Rapids: Eerdmans, 1952–64 [Since published in 4 vols.].

This classic work could qualify as an expositional commentary. Lots of illustration and application for the preacher.

Glynn, *Commentary and Reference Survey*. 10th ed. Grand Rapids: Kregel, 2007.

Glynn gives a helpful list of books regarding homosexuality in Romans 1:21–26 on pages165–66.

Stott, John. *Men Made New*. London: InterVarsity, 1966.

Devotional and homiletical help on Romans 5–8. Originally delivered at the 1965 Keswick Convention. Own and read everything Stott writes.

## SERMONS

Liddon, H. P. *Explanatory Analysis of St. Paul's Epistle to the Romans*. Minneapolis: Klock & Klock, 1977.

A rich and insightful work, it forms the basis of Liddon's expository sermons. Demonstrates the "kind of analysis every preacher should engage in prior to attempting to deliver God's Word," says Barber.

Lloyd-Jones, David Martyn. *Romans*. 14 vols. Edinburgh: Banner of Truth, 2003.

Lloyd-Jones preached these sermons on Friday evenings at Westminster Chapel in London over a period of 13 years! He was an expositor *par excellence* in his generation, though I don't recommend taking 13 years to preach through any book of the Bible! His material is helpful, but he is primarily concerned, like the old Puritans, to extract and explain doctrine wherever he can. This makes for some tedious reading along the way, but no preacher can afford to be without this set when preaching through Romans.

# 1 CORINTHIANS

## EXEGETICAL COMMENTARIES

Garland, David E. *1 Corinthians*. BECNT. Grand Rapids: Baker, 2003.

> Carson ranks this as one of the three best general commentaries on the letter. Garland is a solid expositor thoroughly conversant with the Greek text but concerned as well with theology. This work will be of great help to preachers.

Thiselton, Anthony. *The First Epistle to the Corinthians*. NIGTC. Grand Rapids: Eerdmans, 2000.

> At more 1,400 pages, Thiselton has provided us with one of the most comprehensive works on 1 Corinthians. Attention to Greek syntax, lexicography, sociohistorical background, rhetoric, and history of interpretation, says Bauer. Carson calls it the best commentary on the Greek text of 1 Corinthians.

## EXPOSITORY COMMENTARIES

Barrett, C. K. *The First Epistle to the Corinthians*. HNTC/BNTC. 2nd ed. New York: Harper & Row, 1968.

> Though in some ways surpassed by more recent treatments, this is still a valuable work for the preacher. "Renowned for its lucidity and its comprehensiveness," says Martin. Bauer says, "Clear, concise, insightful, authoritative, and engaging." I agree, but Barrett is not always on the conservative side of things.

Blomberg, Craig L. *1 Corinthians*. NIVAC. Grand Rapids: Zondervan, 1995.

> True to the series, the work focuses on application.

Edwards, Thomas Charles. *A Commentary on the First Epistle to the Corinthians*. Minneapolis: Klock & Klock, 1979.

> "Combines solid exegesis with satisfying exposition ... deserves a place in every pastor's library," says Barber. Though dated, it is still useful.

Fee, Gordon D. *The First Epistle to the Corinthians*. NICNT. Grand Rapids: Eerdmans, 1987.

This continues to rank as one of the best commentaries on 1 Corinthians. Written by a fine New Testament scholar from a Charismatic perspective. Bauer says it is "detailed and learned ... written primarily for those engaged in preaching and teaching in the church." But watch out for his take on 1 Corinthians 14:34–35 as a textual gloss that he claims has no bearing on women's roles in the church. Fee is an egalitarian, devoting 40 pages to 11:2–16 and arguing "head" denotes "source" and not "authority." Fee is a continualist with respect to the gifts.

Godet, F. *Commentary on St. Paul's first epistle to the Corinthians*. Grand Rapids: Kregel, 1977.

I always benefit from reading this conservative French commentator. I learn not only from his head but also from his heart.

Gromacki, Robert. *Called to Be Saints*. Grand Rapids: Baker, 1977.

Excellent short volume from a skilled Greek scholar. Not a verse-by-verse commentary but covers the material section by section with occasional verse-by-verse coverage. This commentary and his 2 Corinthians volume are excellent.

Olshausen, Hermann. *A Commentary on Paul's First and Second Epistles to the Corinthians*. Minneapolis: Klock & Klock, 1984 [1855].

Barber says it "enlivens the sacred page and enriches the spiritual life of the reader." Philip Schaff, the great church historian, praised this volume. Carson thinks it varies between the insightful and the eccentric. I would say more insight here than eccentricity.

Patterson, Paige. *The Troubled, Triumphant Church: An Exposition of 1 Corinthians*. Eugene, OR: Wipf & Stock, 2002.

Patterson, president of Southwestern Baptist Theological Seminary, has a knack for balancing exposition with creative application, and from a thoroughly conservative Baptist perspective. Consult this volume if preaching through the book.

Taylor, Mark. *1 Corinthians*. NAC. Nashville: Broadman & Holman, 2014.

Very fine work from a solid New Testament scholar who teaches at Southwestern Baptist Theological Seminary. Taylor is always judicious and covers all that needs to be covered very well.

Thiselton, Anthony. *1 Corinthians: A Shorter Exegetical and Pastoral Commentary*. Grand Rapids: Eerdmans, 2006.

Drawing on his massive exegetical commentary (see above), but here "combines it afresh with keen practical and pastoral application for readers at all levels." Preachers will be glad to have this volume.

Vaughan, Curtis. *1 Corinthians*. BSC. Grand Rapids: Zondervan, 1983.

See on Romans above.

## SPECIAL STUDIES

Carson, D. A. *Showing the Spirit: A Theological Exposition of 1 Corinthians 12–14*. Grand Rapids: Baker, 1987.

Carson is a continualist on the gifts but is guarded about it.

Edwards, Jonathan. *Charity and its Fruits*. London: Banner of Truth, 1969.

Edwards at his best here, showing us how Christian love works in the life of a Christian.

Jones, John Daniel. *The Greatest of These: An Exposition of 1 Corinthians 13*. London: Hodder & Stoughton, 1925/Klock & Klock, 1982 reprint.

"These are some of the finest expository sermons on 1 Corinthians 13 in print today," says Brookman. Sermons from a British pastor.

Litfin, Duane. *St. Paul's Theology of Proclamation*. Cambridge: Cambridge University Press, 1994.

Excellent treatment of 1 Corinthians 1–4. Don't miss this.

Scroggie, W. Graham. *The Love Life: A Study of 1 Corinthians 13*. London: Pickering & Inglis, 1956.

A brief but helpful devotional treatment by one of my favorite writers of yesteryear.

Smedes, Lewis. *Love Within Limits: Realizing Selfless Love in a Selfish World* [original title, which was later changed to *A Realist's View of 1 Corinthians*]. Grand Rapids: Eerdmans, 1978.

Insights on 1 Corinthians 13 that would be very helpful for the preacher. I first read this book many years ago and liked it very much. Carson calls it "a quiet little gem."

## SERMONS

Redpath, Alan, *The Royal Route to Heaven*. Grand Rapids: Revell, 1993.

Sermons from the warm-hearted former pastor of Moody Memorial Church in Chicago. Read for practical application.

Stedman, Ray. *Expository Studies in 1 Corinthians: The Deep Things of God*. Waco, TX: Word, 1981.

Solid examples of expository preaching. Illustration and application of the text to the church is Stedman's strength. "Highly recommended," says Barber.

Vines, Jerry. *The Corinthian Confusion: A Study of 1 Corinthians*. Published by Jerry Vines Ministries, n.d.

Contains 33 excellent expository sermons from the pen of this master Southern Baptist expositor. Great illustrations.

# 2 CORINTHIANS

## EXEGETICAL COMMENTARIES

Harris, Murray J. *The Second Epistle to the Corinthians*. NIGTC. Grand Rapids: Eerdmans, 2005.

> Theologically conservative all around. Excellent exegesis with a pastoral concern. I always read Harris; he is one of the finest exegetes around.

Thrall, Margaret. T*he Second Epistle to the Corinthians*. 2 vols. ICC. Edinburgh: T. & T. Clark, 1994.

> One of the most detailed exegetical commentaries on the text. Highly technical. Not given to much theological analysis. Thrall does not support the unity of the book, arguing that three separate documents comprise 2 Corinthians.

## EXPOSITORY COMMENTARIES

Barrett, C. K. *The Second Epistle to the Corinthians*. BNTC. Peabody, MA: Hendrickson, 1993.

> See on 1 Corinthians above. Barrett's *2 Corinthians* remains a solid, usable commentary for the preacher.

Barnett, Paul. *The Second Epistle to the Corinthians*. NICNT. Grand Rapids: Eerdmans, 1997.

> This is one of the best works on 2 Corinthians. Readable even for those without any background in Greek. Barnett never loses sight of the role of his passage within the flow of the overall argument. I would consult it regularly if preaching through 2 Corinthians.

Belleville, Linda. *2 Corinthians*. IVPNTC. Downers Grove: InterVarsity, 1996.

> Carson thinks it should be considered a "must" for serious expositors.

Denney, James. *2 Corinthians*. EB. New York: A. C. Armstrong & Son, 1903.

> "Old in years but remarkably fresh and apropos on many issues," says Martin.

Furnish, Victor Paul. *II Corinthians: Translated with Introduction, Notes, and Commentary*. AB. Garden City, NY: Doubleday, 1984.

Furnish was Professor of New Testament at Southern Methodist University's Perkins School of Theology. This is a very detailed work, though from a somewhat liberal perspective. Discerning readers will know what to keep and what to pass over.

Garland, David. *2 Corinthians*. NAC. Nashville: Broadman & Holman, 1999.

One of the stronger volumes in the series. Pastors will find here a solid treatment of the book helpful for exposition.

Gromacki, Robert. *Stand Firm in the Faith: An Exposition of II Corinthians*. Grand Rapids: Baker, 1978.

See under 1 Corinthians above. Don't miss Gromacki's excellent treatment of 5:14–21. He traces the argument and understands Paul's theology here better than most.

Hafemann, Scott J. *2 Corinthians*. NIVAC. Grand Rapids: Zondervan, 2000.

This is one of the stronger volumes in the NIVAC series. Balanced exposition and application.

Harris, Murray J. *2 Corinthians*. REBC 11. Grand Rapids: Zondervan, 2008.

Short but a masterpiece of condensed style, says Moo. Harris wrote his Ph.D. dissertation on 2 Corinthians 5:1–10. He taught at Trinity Evangelical Divinity School for years. I always try to read anything Harris writes.

Kent, Homer Austin. *A Heart Opened Wide: Studies in II Corinthians*. NTS. Grand Rapids: Baker, 1982.

Kent will provide preachers with grist for their homiletical mill. Written in a popular style and majors on application.

Kruse, Colin. *The Second Epistle of Paul to the Corinthians*. TNTC. Grand Rapids: Eerdmans, 1987.

Excellent, concise treatment of the letter. Helpful for expositors.

Martin, Ralph. *2 Corinthians*. WBC. Waco, TX: Word, 1986.

Considered a solid, detailed treatment of 2 Corinthians, this is the fruit of many years of research. Martin was a colleague of F. F. Bruce at Manchester in the late 1960s and Professor of New Testament at Fuller Seminary until his retirement in 1988. Martin served as editor of WBC and contributed the James volume to the series as well.

## SPECIAL STUDIES

Carson, D. A. *From Triumphalism to Maturity: An Exposition of 2 Corinthians 10–13.* Grand Rapids: Baker, 1984/Reissued by Baker in 2007 under the title *A Model of Christian Maturity.*

Helpful treatment of these famous four chapters where Paul lets his hair down and bares his heart.

Savage, Timothy. *Power Through Weakness: Paul's Understanding of Christian Ministry in 2 Corinthians.* SNTSMS 86. New York: Cambridge University Press, 1996.

The title says it all.

## SERMONS

Duduit, Michael. *Joy in Ministry: Messages from 2 Corinthians.* Grand Rapids: Baker, 1989.

Duduit is the editor of Preaching Magazine and organizer of the annual National Conference on Preaching. Here are 20 very helpful expository messages.

Redpath, Alan. *Blessings out of Buffetings: Studies in II Corinthians.* Westwood, NJ: Revell, 1965.

Redpath was a pastor of Moody Memorial Church in Chicago. These sermons are practically oriented.

Robertson, F. W. *Expository Lectures on St. Paul's Epistles to the Corinthians.* London: Smith, Elder, and Co., 1859.

These expositions were given on Sunday afternoons at Trinity Chapel, Brighton, where Robertson was the pastor from 1847–1853. Robertson became far more famous after his death with the publication of his sermons. Here are 34 messages on 1 Corinthians and 26 messages on 2 Corinthians. Worth your time!

Stedman, Ray. *Expository Studies in 2 Corinthians: Power Out of Weakness.* Waco, TX: Word, 1982.

See above under 1 Corinthians above.

# GALATIANS

**EXEGETICAL COMMENTARIES**

Bruce, F. F. *The Epistle to the Galatians*. NIGTC. Grand Rapids: Eerdmans, 1982.

> Bruce never complicates or oversimplifies. He is always a steady Antares for the preacher.

Eadie, John. *A Commentary on the Greek Text of the Epistle of Paul to the Galatians*. Edinburgh: T. & T. Clark, 1869.

> See under Ephesians.

Lightfoot, Joseph Barber. *The Epistle of St. Paul to the Galatians*. Grand Rapids: Zondervan, 1966.

> Regarded as a classic. Hendrickson Publishers has combined his Galatians, Philippians, Colossians, and Philemon commentaries in one volume [1981]. Without question, one of the greatest commentaries on the Greek text of Galatians, says Barber.

Moo, Douglas J. *Galatians*. BECNT. Grand Rapids: Baker, 2013.

> From the prolific pen of the professor of New Testament at Wheaton College Graduate School, this might well be ranked as the best exegetical commentary available on Galatians. A work of painstaking exegesis combined with serious theological reflection. Moo is fair and balanced in the presentation of alternative views, including the New Perspective on Paul. The prose is easily readable for all. You cannot afford to be without this volume!

Schreiner, Thomas. *Galatians*. ZECNT. Grand Rapids: Zondervan, 2010.

> Schreiner has written an exegetical volume that will not overwhelm the pastor in the minutiae of details. By all means consult it if preaching through Galatians.

Silva, Moises. *Interpreting Galatians: Explorations in Exegetical Method*. 2nd ed. Grand Rapids: Baker, 2001.

> Wide-ranging, semi-technical work that covers aspects of the history of interpretation, key exegetical issues in the text, background and date, and Paul's theology.

# EXPOSITORY COMMENTARIES

Fung, Ronald Y. K. *The Epistle to the Galatians*. NICNT. Grand Rapids: Eerdmans, 1988.

> Replaces the Ridderbos volume in the series. A work very helpful to preachers in the tradition of the NIC series. Carson calls it "workmanlike."

George, Timothy. *Galatians*. NAC. Nashville: Broadman & Holman, 1994.

> Many consider this to be the best volume on a New Testament book in the NAC series. I certainly would not argue differently. Its major strength is its survey of interpretation of Galatians, especially from the Reformation forward. The exposition is succinct, clear, and on point. Pastors cannot afford to ignore this volume when preaching through Galatians.

Gromacki, Robert. *Stand Fast in Liberty: An Exposition of Galatians*. Grand Rapids: Baker, 1979.

> Gromacki packs muscle in small places. He was professor of Bible and Greek at Cedarville University in Ohio. This brief work, and all of his commentaries, is worth the preacher's time and use.

Longenecker, Richard. *Galatians*. WBC. Dallas: Word, 1990.

> Longenecker has always favored Galatians, and this volume is the fruit of serious study. While probably of less interest to most preachers, one strength of this work is its strong introduction dealing with the history of the debate over destination. Longenecker makes a good effort at synthesizing the main theological issues. Detailed (over 70 pages of introduction) but useful.

Luther, Martin. *Commentary on Galatians*. Grand Rapids: Kregel, 1979 reprint of the 1850 edition.

> This is an abridged volume. If you want the whole, consult volumes 26 and 27 in *Luther's Works* in the Concordia edition. If you have the time, take a gander at Luther and be inspired!

McKnight, Scot. *Galatians*. NIVAC. Grand Rapids: Zondervan, 1995.

> This volume by a gifted New Testament Arminian scholar will be very helpful to pastors preaching through Galatians. As the series intends, it focuses strongly on application.

Vaughan, Curtis. *Galatians*. SGC. Grand Rapids: Zondervan, 1972.

> See under Romans above.

Witherington, Ben, III. *Grace in Galatia: A Commentary on Paul's Letter to the Galatians*. Grand Rapids: Eerdmans, 1998.

The strength of this work is Witherington's analysis of the overall rhetorical macrostructure of the book and its concomitant sociological background. One helpful aspect of this work for preachers is each chapter concludes with a consideration for contemporary application.

## SPECIAL STUDIES

Barclay, William. *Flesh and Spirit: An Examination of Galatians 5:19–23*. Nashville: Abingdon, 1962.

Great word studies on this passage that contrasts the works of the flesh and the fruit of the Spirit. Can't be without this one when preaching on this passage.

## SERMONS

Stott, John. *The Message of the Galatians: Only One Way*. BST: Downers Grove: InterVarsity, 1968.

Rich expository messages from this evangelical Anglican master expositor.

# EPHESIANS

## EXEGETICAL COMMENTARIES

Arnold, Clinton E. *Ephesians*. ZECNT. Grand Rapid: Zondervan, 2010.

Solid on exegetical help and includes several pastoral suggestions.

Best, Earnest. *Ephesians*. ICC. Edinburgh: T. & T. Clark, 1998.

Must be ranked as one of the top-of-the-line modern exegetical commentaries on the book. The introduction is almost 100 pages and the commentary covers over 550 pages. Best is the emeritus professor of divinity and biblical criticism at the University of Glasgow.

Eadie, John. *A Commentary on the Greek Text of the Epistle of Paul to the Ephesians*. 2nd ed. Grand Rapids: Baker, 1979 reprint.

Smith considered it one of the most satisfying commentaries strictly devoted to the interpretation of the text. Hodge, Ellicott, and many others praised this volume. The Scottish Eadie served as a pastor for 41 years, and in his early 30s became chairman of the Department of Biblical Literature in the Divinity Hall of the University of Glasgow. Eadie also wrote commentaries on Galatians, Philippians, Colossians, and 1 and 2 Thessalonians, all of which should be in your library. Though his exegesis is dated, his pastoral heart and devotional spirit isn't.

Hoehner, Harold. *Ephesians: An Exegetical Commentary*. Grand Rapids: Baker, 2002.

Weighing in at more than 900 pages, this is the most extensive commentary on Ephesians available. Hagner called it "A tour de force." Hoehner taught New Testament at Dallas Theological Seminary for more than 30 years. Moo said of this work: "One of the best commentaries on Ephesians in English. Hoehner's breadth of research, detail on critical issues, and solid exegetical treatment are impressive." Indeed.

Lincoln, Andrew. *Ephesians*. WBC. Dallas: Word, 1990.

Good, detailed exegesis but overly enthralled with redaction criticism. Denies Pauline authorship. Lincoln attempts to deal with the theology of the book, but like most of the volumes in the WBC series, there is little or no emphasis on application. Still a helpful volume.

Robinson, J. Armitage. *St. Paul's Epistle to the Ephesians*. 2nd ed. London: James Clarke, 1904.

A 300-page exegetical study that is still very valuable today. Contains 120 pages of exposition without use of the Greek, then 160 pages of very exacting exegetical analysis, including 10 important excurses on the meaning of key Greek terms. Watch for his helpful paraphrase of the Greek text as well. This work is still considered a classic on Ephesians.

Thielman, Frank. *Ephesians*. BECNT. Grand Rapids: Baker, 2010.

> The readable style of this commentary will make it helpful to pastors who have not had much Greek. Careful exegesis and theological treatment, along with application. "A model of informed and lucid interpretation," says Brian Rosner.

Westcott, B. F. *St. Paul's Epistle to the Ephesians*. Grand Rapids: Eerdmans, 1958 [1906].

> In-depth exegetical work by the famed Greek scholar and Bishop of Durham, England. Always helpful on the Greek text.

## EXPOSITORY COMMENTARIES

Bruce, F. F. *The Epistles to the Colossians, to Philemon and to the Ephesians*. NICNT. Grand Rapids: Eerdmans, 1984.

> Bruce is always reliable and will be of help to the preacher.

Kent, Homer. *Ephesians: The Glory of the Church*. Chicago: Moody, 1971.

> Soundly expository in approach, there is much help here for the preacher. Kent's work is expositional and practical.

Klein, William W. *Ephesians*. REBC 12. Grand Rapids: Zondervan, 2006.

> The EBC series has a stellar reputation for solid biblical exposition without being too technical. Klein's work on Ephesians is an excellent resource for pastors preaching through the book.

Liefeld, Walter. *Ephesians*. IVPNTC. Downers Grove: InterVarsity, 1997.

> "Packs a lifetime of thoughtful study of this epistle into a very small space," says Carson. Liefeld authored a volume entitled *New Testament Exposition: From Text to Sermon* that should be in every preacher's library.

O'Brien, Peter T. *The Letter to the Ephesians*. PNTC. Grand Rapids: Eerdmans, 1999.

> An excellent work that should be used when preaching through Hebrews. Carson thinks it likely the best English language commentary for pastors.

Snodgrass, Klyne. *Ephesians*. NIVAC. Grand Rapids: Zondervan, 1996.

> Snodgrass fulfills the series' intent: taking us from the biblical text to contemporary life.

Stott, John. *The Message of Ephesians: God's New Society*. Downers Grove: InterVarsity, 1979.

> Stott is always helpful to the pastor. He packs more judicious comment in a short space than most. Stott was a pastor/scholar whose works should be in every pastor's library.

Vaughan, Curtis. *Ephesians*. SGC. Grand Rapids: Zondervan, 1977.

> See under Romans above.

## DEVOTIONAL COMMENTARIES

Moule, H. C. G. *Ephesians Studies: Lessons in Faith and Walk*. 2nd ed. Grand Rapids: Zondervan, 1900.

> Reprinted by Kregel in 1977 under the title *Ephesians*. Barber calls this "a devotional masterpiece." He is correct.

## SERMONS

Criswell, W. A. *Ephesians: An Exposition*. Grand Rapids: Zondervan, 1974.

> Helpful sermons, mostly expository, loaded with good illustrations.

Dale, R. W. *The Epistle to the Ephesians: Its Doctrine and Ethics*. 3rd ed. London: Hodder & Stoughton, 1887.

> Twenty-four expository sermons from the famous pastor of Carr's Lane Church in London. Dale was a very good communicator.

Ironside, Henry. *In the Heavenlies: Practical Expository Addresses on the Epistle to the Ephesians*. New York: Loizeaux, 1937.

> All of Ironside's commentaries are worth owning for homiletical purposes, but this is definitely one of his best.

Lloyd-Jones, David Martyn. *Expositions on Ephesians*. Eight volumes under various individual titles. Grand Rapids: Baker, 1972–82.

> This is a classic series of sermons from the renowned pastor of Westminster Chapel in London. Not to be missed!

Parker, Joseph. *The Epistle to the Ephesians*. Grand Rapids: Baker, 1956.

> Expositional and practical sermons on Ephesians from the famed Congregational pastor and contemporary of Spurgeon. His pulpit eloquence is reflected in these messages. His sermons are found in the 27-volume *The People's Bible*, which would be worth a look from time to time.

Pattison, R. E. and H. C. G. Moule. *Exposition of Ephesians: Lessons in Grace and Godliness*. Minneapolis: Klock & Klock, 1983.

Here is Pattison's commentary on Ephesians and Moule's expository messages on Ephesians combined.

# PHILIPPIANS

## EXEGETICAL COMMENTARIES

Eadie, John. *Commentary on the Greek Text of the Epistle of Paul to the Philippians*. Grand Rapids: Zondervan, 1992.

Eadie can't be beaten when it comes to treatment of the key Greek words in the text. Also contains one of the most comprehensive discussions of Phil. 2:5–11.

Lightfoot, J. B. *St. Paul's Epistle to the Philippians*. Grand Rapids: Zondervan, 1953.

Barber calls this a "thorough exposition which discusses every grammatical and interpretive problem imaginable."

O'Brien, Peter T. *The Epistle to the Philippians*. NIGTC. Grand Rapids: Eerdmans, 1991.

My choice for the best exegetical commentary. O'Brien offers a solid thematic and theological analysis of each passage.

## EXPOSITORY COMMENTARIES

Bruce, F. F. *Philippians*. NICNT. Peabody, MA: Hendrickson, 1989.

See above under Ephesians.

Collange, Jean-Francois. *Philippians*. Eugene, OR: Wipf & Stock, 2009.

English translation of his 1973 commentary in French. Excellent treatment with lots of good help for preachers. "A mine of information and inspiration for the preacher's study," says Martin.

Fee, Gordon D. *Paul's Letter to the Philippians*. NICNT. Grand Rapids: Eerdmans, 1995.

Fee is imminently readable and a good exegete. Good exposition of the text here with detailed technical matters relegated to the footnotes. Very helpful to the pastor.

Garland, David E. *Philippians*. REBC 12. Grand Rapids: Zondervan, 2006.

"Frequently insightful," says Carson. Garland always provides a steady expository diet.

Greenlee, J. Harold. *An Exegetical Summary of Philippians*. 2nd ed. Dallas: SIL International, 2008.

See under Abernathy on Romans above for this series.

Gromacki, Robert. *Stand United in Joy: An Exposition of Philippians*. Grand Rapids: Baker, 1980.

See under Galatians above.

Hansen, G. Walter. *The Letter to the Philippians*. PNTC. Grand Rapids: Eerdmans, 2009.

Solidly conservative. Helpful introduction and bibliography, followed by satisfying exposition. Workmanlike; 350 pages. Preachers will want to use this volume.

Hawthorne, Gerald and Ralph Martin. *Philippians*. WBC. 2nd ed. Nashville: Thomas Nelson, 2004.

This 2004 revised edition of Hawthorne's 1983 volume by Ralph Martin is a welcome addition to the series. Expands the original by more than 100 pages. Copious notes and bibliography attached to each section.

Johnstone, Robert. *Lectures Exegetical and Practical on The Epistle of Paul to the Philippians*. Grand Rapids: Baker, 1955 reprint [1875].

Barber calls it "a thorough, practical, and homiletical exposition."

Martin, Ralph. *Philippians*. TNTC. 2nd ed. Revised. Grand Rapids: Eerdmans, 2004.

Concise yet meaty treatment, per the TNTC's goal.

Melick, Richard. *Philippians, Colossians, and Philemon*. NAC. Nashville: Broadman & Holman, 1991.

One of the earliest volumes released in the series but a good, solid treatment that will be helpful to pastors.

Silva, Moises. *Philippians*. BECNT. 2nd ed. Grand Rapids: Baker, 2005.

Silva is a prolific author and solid New Testament interpreter with a linguistics background (he did graduate work in Semitics at Dropsie College). The commentary transliterates all Greek in the body, and each section is followed by "Additional Notes"—short exegetical notes on aspects of the Greek text that shed further light on the passage.

Thielman, Frank. *Philippians*. NIVAC. Grand Rapids: Zondervan, 1995.

Good balance between exposition and application by a recognized New Testament scholar.

## DEVOTIONAL COMMENTARIES

Jowett, John. *The High Calling: Meditations on St. Paul's Letter to the Philippians*. London: Andrew Melrose, 1909.

Thoughtful and heart-warming studies of Philippians containing excellent preaching material from the pastor who preceded G. Campbell Morgan at the famous Westminster Chapel in London.

Moule, H. C. G. *Philippians*. Grand Rapids: Kregel, 1977 reprint.

Devotional treatment in beautiful prose with a focus on application. Not to be missed.

Rees, Paul. *The Adequate Man: Studies in Philippians*. London: Marshall, Morgan & Scott, 1958.

Rich, sermonic, and devotional studies with suggested sermon outlines, loads of illustrations and practical application. Preachers will find homiletical help here.

Robertson, A. T. *Paul's Joy in Christ*. Grand Rapids: Baker, 1979 reprint.

From the pen of the renowned Southern Baptist Greek scholar, this work brings insights on the text and ideas to the preacher.

Vaughan, C. J. *Epistle to the Philippians*. Minneapolis: Klock & Klock, 1979.

Vaughan has an amazing talent for developing expository messages based on his detailed exegesis of the Greek. Many consider these expository messages a classic. I still find Vaughan valuable today.

## SPECIAL STUDIES

Martin, Ralph. *Carmen Christi: Philippians 2:5–11 in Recent Interpretation and in the Setting of Early Christian Worship*. Revised ed. Grand Rapids: Eerdmans, 1983.

Excellent treatment of one of the four great Christological passages in the New Testament. A classic that should be in your library.

## SERMONS

Boice, James M. *Philippians*. Grand Rapids: Baker, 1971.

Boice was the pastor of the famed Tenth Presbyterian Church in Philadelphia. He was a noted expositor, and his sermons are always worth your read. All of his commentaries are basically his expositions preached in his church.

Lloyd-Jones, David Martyn. *The Life of Joy: Philippians*. 2 vols. Grand Rapids: Baker, 1993.

These sermons were preached in Westminster Chapel, where Lloyd-Jones was the pastor from 1947–1968.

Motyer, J. A. *Philippian Studies: The Richness of Christ*. Chicago: InterVarsity Press, 1966.

These are essentially sermons delivered by Motyer in the chapel of Clifton Theological College and were further used at the morning Bible Readings at Webster Memorial Church, Kingston, Jamaica in 1965. These are well worth your reading, first, for your own spiritual enrichment, and second, for your sermon preparation. Motyer has since published extensively, especially on Isaiah.

# COLOSSIANS & PHILEMON

## EXEGETICAL COMMENTARIES

Barth, Markus and Helmut Blanke. *The Letter to Philemon*. Grand
  Rapids: Eerdmans, 2000.

> I've had it in my library since it came out but still have not finished
> reading its 561 pages! No doubt the most comprehensive work on
> Philemon. The authors demonstrate their knowledge of the ancient world
> with respect to slavery. Verse by verse in approach, with several helpful
> excurses dealing with issues historical and theological.

Dunn, James D. G. *The Epistles to the Colossians and to Philemon*. NIGTC.
  Grand Rapids: Eerdmans, 1996.

> Dunn was for many years the Lightfoot Professor of Divinity at the
> University of Durham. Known for his support of the so-called "New
> Perspective" on Paul. Harris says of this volume: "... characteristic
> attention to detail, mastery of ancient parallels and modern scholarship,
> and grasp of theological issues." The exegesis is geared toward a
> theological interpretation of the book.

Eadie, John. *Commentary on the Epistle of Paul to the Colossians*. Grand
  Rapids: Zondervan, 1957.

> This 19th-century commentator is always informative. Based on the
> Greek text but rich in exposition.

Harris, Murray. *Colossians & Philemon*. EGGNT. Nashville: Broadman
  & Holman, 2010.

> First published in 1991, Harris delivers beautifully. All volumes in this
> series have a brief introduction, list of recommended commentaries,
> extensive exegetical notes, translation and expanded paraphrase of
> the book, comprehensive exegetical outline, homiletical outlines, and a
> glossary of grammatical and rhetorical terms. Extremely helpful. Harris
> is professor emeritus of New Testament exegesis and theology at Trinity
> and former warden of Tyndale House in Cambridge.

Lightfoot, J. B. *St. Paul's Epistle to the Colossians and to Philemon*. Grand
  Rapids: Zondervan, 1959.

> Based on the Greek text. The third of the great Greek 19th-century
> triumvirate Hort and Westcott, Lightfoot's work is dated yet not
> antiquated. Erudite and insightful, according to Bauer.

O'Brien, Peter. *Colossians, Philemon*. WBC. Waco, TX: Word, 1982.

> O'Brien has established himself as one of the premier New Testament commentators. His work is generally thorough, judicious, and conservative in outlook. Well considers the history of interpretation but also synthesizes the theology of each passage. "The explanation section synthesizes the theology of the passage and explores its significance for the religious experience of the original readers," says Bauer. I always try to read O'Brien if I can.

Pao, David W. *Colossians and Philemon*. ZECNT. Grand Rapids: Zondervan, 2012.

> Written for pastors but makes serious use of the Greek text. Pao succeeds in meeting the series' goal: exegete each passage succinctly in its grammatical, literary, and historical context.

## EXPOSITORY COMMENTARIES

Barclay, William. *The Letters to the Philippians, Colossians, and Thessalonians*. Revised ed. DSB. Philadelphia: Westminster, 1975.

> See below on Hebrews. Word studies and illustrations galore!

Bruce, F. F. *The Epistles to the Colossians, to Philemon and to the Ephesians*. NICNT. Grand Rapids: Eerdmans, 1984.

> See above on Ephesians.

Garland, David E. *Colossians and Philemon*. NIVAC. Grand Rapids: Zondervan, 1998.

> Garland treats Colossians in 250 pages and Philemon in just over 80 pages. He presents a good balance between exposition and application, as the series intends.

Gromacki, Robert. *Stand Perfect in Wisdom: An Exposition of Colossians and Philemon*. Grand Rapids: Baker, 1981.

> See above on Galatians.

Moo, Douglas J. *The Letters to the Colossians and to Philemon*. PNTC. Grand Rapids: Eerdmans, 2008.

> Moo interacts with the Greek text but explains the English text in a clear way. Blomberg says this book should be the first choice of most pastors and teachers because it is not unnecessarily long.

Moule, H. C. G. *Colossians and Philemon Studies: Lessons in Faith and Holiness*. Grand Rapids: Zondervan, 1962.

> A minor classic by a major exegete. Excellent exposition and application couched in a devotional style.

Vaughan, Curtis. *Colossians*. EBC 11. Grand Rapids: Zondervan, 1978.

> See above on Romans. See also Vaughan's *Colossians and Philemon* in the BSC series, 1981. Anything Vaughan writes is worth reading. He taught Greek at Southwestern Baptist Theological Seminary for many years and was my favorite professor when I was a student there.

## DEVOTIONAL COMMENTARIES

Scroggie, W. Graham. *Studies in Philemon*. Grand Rapids: Kregel, 1982.

> Formerly titled *A Note to a Friend* [1927], "this work remains one of the best ever written on Philemon," according to Barber.

## SPECIAL STUDIES

Petersen, Norman. *Rediscovering Paul: Philemon and the Sociology of Paul's Narrative World*. Philadelphia: Fortress, 1985.

> Employs contemporary literary and sociological study to Philemon, with moderate success. Consult if you have extra time.

## SERMONS

Ironside, Henry. *Charge that to My Account*. Chicago: Moody, 1931.

> Excellent homiletical and practical treatment of Philemon, enriched with excellent illustrations.

Maclaren, Alexander. *The Epistles of St. Paul to the Colossians and Philemon*. EB. New York: A. C. Armstrong & Son, 1903.

> Considered one of Maclaren's best and one of the best volumes in the EB series. "A masterpiece of scholarship and exposition," says Wiersbe.

Nicholson, W. R. *Oneness with Christ: Popular Studies in the Epistle to the Colossians*. Grand Rapids: Kregel, 1903.

> Nicholson was a bishop in the Reformed Episcopal Church and dean and professor of exegesis and pastoral theology until his death in 1901. He was a remarkable biblical expositor and preacher of the last part of the 19th century. This work does not cover the entire letter, but what is covered is pure gold.

# 1 & 2 THESSALONIANS

## EXEGETICAL COMMENTARIES

Eadie, John. *A Commentary on the Greek Text of the Epistle of Paul to the Thessalonians*. Minneapolis: James and Klock, 1977 [1877].

See on Ephesians above.

Shogren, Gary. *1 and 2 Thessalonians*. ZECNT. Grand Rapids: Zondervan, 2012.

Shogren is professor of New Testament at Seminario ESEPA, San Jose, Costa Rica. He gives his own translation from the Greek text and traces the literary structure well. The commentary is verse by verse, with exegetical outlines and theology in application sections that are most helpful to pastors. The graphical displays in this series are very helpful to preachers as well.

Wanamaker, Charles A. *The Epistles to the Thessalonians*. NIGTC. Grand Rapids: Eerdmans, 1990.

Strong focus on Greek exegesis, historical and literary analysis, coupled with theological analysis. Bauer says it is the first commentary to integrate historical-critical methods with social-scientific and rhetorical approaches. But watch out for his reversal of the chronological order of the books.

## EXPOSITIONAL COMMENTARIES

Bruce, F. F. *1 & 2 Thessalonians*. WBC. Waco, TX: Word, 1982.

A careful and detailed exposition as we have come to expect from the pen of this venerable British conservative scholar. Helpful background articles ranging from Christianity in Macedonia to the antichrist.

Fee, Gordon D. *The First and Second Letters to the Thessalonians*. NICNT. Grand Rapids: Eerdmans, 2009.

See on Fee under 1 Corinthians above. This is a solid work in the NIC series that would be helpful to the pastor.

Green, Gene L. *The Letters to the Thessalonians*. PNTC. Grand Rapids: Eerdmans, 2002.

In-depth introduction covering all aspects of Thessalonica and its people. A verse-by-verse, exegetically detailed, and expository treatment that excels in the attempt to bridge the gap between then and now. Preachers will find it useful.

Hiebert, D. Edmond. *1 & 2 Thessalonians*. Revised edition. Chicago: Moody, 1992.

Hiebert is one of my favorite commentators. His work is non-technical yet stays close to the text in exposition. He is ideal for pastors.

Marshall, I. Howard. *1 and 2 Thessalonians*. NCBC. Grand Rapids: Eerdmans, 1983.

Solid exegesis as we've come to expect from Marshall. "Concise, straightforward, accessible to the nonspecialist," says Bauer. Some application here as well.

Martin, D. Michael. *1 & 2 Thessalonians*. NAC. Nashville: Broadman & Holman, 1995.

Sound exposition, clear presentation, appropriate application.

Morris, Leon. *The First and Second Epistles to the Thessalonians*. NICNT. Revised ed. Grand Rapids: Eerdmans, 2006.

You just can't go wrong with Morris. Excellent introduction, solid exegesis, relevant application. The treatment is paragraph by paragraph. Reformed perspective. See also his volume on the epistles in the Word Biblical Themes series [1989].

Thomas, Robert L. *1 & 2 Thessalonians*. REBC 12. Grand Rapids: Zondervan, 2006.

A very accessible, brief but workmanlike treatment that is helpful for preachers.

Ward, Ronald. *Commentary on 1 & 2 Thessalonians*. Waco, TX: Word, 1974.

Formerly a professor of New Testament at Wycliffe College in Toronto and then a rector and Rural Dean in Canada, Ward has knack for taking complicated things and making them simple for all. About his commentaries, he said: "I sought to attain academic respectability and practical utility. Prominent in my mind were preachers and teachers who needed help. I stand where they stand and have therefore tried to be vivid and 'illustrate.' A commentary gives its author the authority to comment, and this liberty has been taken. ... At times a comment may not be precisely relevant to the text, but it should be relevant to the situation of the preacher or teacher who is studying the text." Wise words. Based on the RSV text, this work is indeed helpful to preachers. See his companion volume on 1 and 2 Timothy, and don't miss his *Royal Sacrament: The Preacher and His Message*. Once I began reading this book, I could hardly put it down. Excellent!

## DEVOTIONAL COMMENTARIES

Marsh, F. E. *Practical Truths from First Thessalonians*. Grand Rapids: Kregel, 1986.

Marsh (1858–1931) conducted a lifetime teaching ministry. His books are biblically steeped and practically and devotionally oriented. This work combines expository and illustrative material that will be very helpful to the preacher. 27 chapters covering 1 Thessalonians 1–3. Consult it before you preach on 1 Thessalonians!

## SPECIAL STUDIES

Weima, Jeffrey and Stanley Porter. *An Annotated Bibliography of 1 and 2 Thessalonians*. New Testament Studies and Tools 26. Leiden: Brill, 1998.

Everything you ever wanted to know about books on the Thessalonian letters through 1998.

## SERMONS

Ockenga, Harold John. *The Church in God*. Westwood, NJ: Revell, 1956.

Expository sermons by this leader of post-WWII evangelicalism.

# 1 & 2 TIMOTHY AND TITUS

## EXEGETICAL COMMENTARIES

Knight, George W., III. *The Pastoral Epistles*. NIGTC. Grand Rapids: Eerdmans, 1992.

> Argues for Pauline authorship with Lukan amanuensis. Detailed emphasis on exegesis, as the series intends. The approach is verse by verse, but structure and theology are not neglected. No real focus on application. I would consider this a must-have volume for serious exegesis.

Marshall, I. Howard. *The Pastoral Epistles*. ICC. Edinburgh: T. & T. Clark, 1999.

> An 850-page, in-depth study of the pastorals from the pen of the venerable professor of New Testament exegesis at the University of Aberdeen. Here is Marshall at his best. This is a must-have volume for exegetical treatment. My two major concerns are Marshall's rejection of Pauline authorship and his treatment of 1 Timothy 2 on women teaching men in church as being culturally bound. But just eat around these bones and enjoy the rest of the meal. Another must-have volume for serious exegesis.

Mounce, William. *Pastoral Epistles*. WBC. Nashville: Thomas Nelson, 2000.

> Excellent exegetical/expository treatment from this Greek scholar. Accepts Pauline authorship. Hefty bibliography on each passage. Good focus on the theology of the letters but little attention to application.

Towner, Philip H. *The Letters to Timothy and Titus*. NICNT. Grand Rapids: Eerdmans, 2006.

> Towner's 886 pages may be the most useful commentary for pastors that is based on the Greek text. Accepts Pauline authorship, but watch out for his odd take on 1 Timothy 2:8–15.

## EXPOSITIONAL COMMENTARIES

Fairbairn, Patrick. *The Pastoral Epistles*. Minneapolis: James and Klock, 1976.

> This classic reprint from a 19th-century Scottish pastor/theologian is the fruit of his many years of teaching pastoral ministry to advanced ministerial students. Very worthwhile.

Guthrie, Donald. *The Pastoral Epistles*. TNTC. 2nd ed. Grand Rapids: Eerdmans, 2007.

Hendriksen, William. *1 and 2 Timothy and Titus*. Grand Rapids: Baker, 1957.

I consider this to be one of the strongest volumes in the series Hendriksen wrote. A good, expository treatment helpful to pastors.

Hiebert, D. Edmond. *Titus*. EBC 11. Grand Rapids: Zondervan, 1978.

Hiebert will always be beneficial to the pastor, especially those without knowledge of Greek. He is always strong on detailed outlines.

Johnson, Luke Timothy. *The First and Second Letters to Timothy*. AB. New York: Doubleday, 2001.

Johnson is a relatively conservative Catholic scholar who argues for Pauline authorship. One major strength of this work is the introduction, which covers the history of interpretation from the Fathers for interested readers. Serious linguistic analysis, theological reflection, and even some application.

Kelly, J. N. D. *A Commentary on the Pastoral Epistles*. Grand Rapids: Baker, 1978 reprint.

Kelly provides his own translation from the Greek but then produces a readable exposition. Argues for Pauline authorship. Kelly was principal of St. Edmund Hall, Oxford, from 1951 until his retirement in 1979. C. K. Barrett said of this work: "An excellent book in every way. The exposition in particular is sheer pleasure to study ... detailed discussion of the various interpretations ... with an easy but dignified style."

Kent, Homer. *The Pastoral Epistles*. Revised ed. Chicago: Moody, 1982.

Here is a careful, detailed but not overly technical exposition designed for pastors. Scholarly but readable. Weds the exposition and practical together. Very useful for the pastor. Kent was president of Grace College and Grace Theological Seminary.

Köstenberger, Andreas J. *1 & 2 Timothy and Titus*. REBC 12. Grand Rapids: Zondervan, 2006.

Köstenberger always comes through with solid exposition for the preacher.

Lea, Thomas and Hayne Griffin. *1 & 2 Timothy and Titus*. NAC. Nashville: Broadman & Holman, 1992.

A good, basic treatment of the text that would stand in good stead for pastors.

Liddon, H. P. *Explanatory Analysis of St. Paul's First Epistle to Timothy*. Minneapolis: Klock & Klock, 1978.

Excellent analytical material with careful attention to the Greek text from this 19th-century, one-time professor of New Testament exegesis at Oxford and for 20 years the famed pastor of St. Paul's Cathedral, London.

Stott, John. *The Message of 2 Timothy: Guard the Gospel*. BST. Downers Grove: InterVarsity, 1999.

See also his *The Message of 1 Timothy & Titus: God's Good News for the World*. BST. Downers Grove: InterVarsity, 1996.

Ward, Ronald. *Commentary on 1 & 2 Timothy*. Waco, TX: Word, 1974.

See on 1 and 2 Thessalonians above.

## DEVOTIONAL COMMENTARIES

Stock, Eugene. *Practical Truths from the Pastoral Epistles*. Grand Rapids: Kregel, 1983.

Stock (1836–1928) was one of the most well-read individuals of his day, yet he had such a knack for distilling the essence of things and presenting it in a way that benefits scholars, pastors, and laymen. "No book on pastoral theology, based on the Pastoral Epistles, contains more solid scholarship, more practical application, and is more of a delight to read," says Wiersbe.

Chadwick, W. Edward. *Pastoral Teaching of Paul*. Grand Rapids: Kregel, 1984.

Approaching Paul as a great pastor, Chadwick gleans from the Apostle's ministry in Acts and his Pastoral Epistles, and clear and compelling prose relates them to modern day pastor/preachers. Chapter titles include: "The Minister of Christ, a Workman;" "The Pastor and His Pastorate;" "Concepts of Ministry;" "The Love of Souls;" "The Motive Power of Ministry;" "The Prayers of Paul;" and "Paul on Preaching." Wiersbe wrote the introduction and commends it highly.

Moule, H. C. G. *Studies in II Timothy*. Grand Rapids: Kregel, 1977.

First published in 1905, it is a devotional classic.

## SPECIAL STUDIES

Köstenberger, Andreas J. and Terry Wilder. *Entrusted with the Gospel: Paul's Theology in the Pastoral Epistles*. Nashville: Broadman & Holman, 2010.

This work by two trusted New Testament scholars would be of immense help to pastors preaching through the letters.

## SERMONS

Draper, James. *Titus: Patterns for Church Living*. Wheaton: Tyndale, 1978.

Expository messages preached at the First Baptist Church, Euless, TX, when Draper was pastor there. Very helpful homiletical material.

# HEBREWS

## EXEGETICAL COMMENTARIES

Delitzsch, Franz. *Commentary on the Epistle to the Hebrews*. 2 vols. Minneapolis: Klock & Klock, 1978 [1871].

> From the pen of the renowned Lutheran scholar and Jewish Christian, this is a classic treatment of Hebrews still valuable today. Delitzsch was conservative; a brilliant scholar with a warm heart. He argued Luke was the author of Hebrews ... so he has to be on the ball!

Ellingworth, Paul. *The Epistle to the Hebrews*. NIGTC. Grand Rapids: Eerdmans, 1993.

> Ellingworth's volume is still considered the top-of-the-line Greek exegetical treatment of Hebrews. It is detailed but contains less theological analysis than Lane, who should be consulted in conjunction with Ellingworth. Slim treatment of the thorny passage Hebrews 6:4–6.

Lane, William. *Hebrews*. WBC. 2 vols. Dallas: Word, 1991.

> One of the top five commentaries on Hebrews from the pen of this Baptist scholar who loved working on this book. Lengthy introduction covers the waterfront well and reflects knowledge of and interest in discourse analysis in analyzing structure. Weds exegesis and theology together that is helpful for preachers. Don't miss Lane's more popular commentary on Hebrews, *Call to Commitment: Responding to the Message of Hebrews*. Peabody, MA: Hendrickson, 1985; Regent College, 2004 reprint.

Miller, Neva. *The Epistle to the Hebrews: An Analytical and Exegetical Handbook*. Dallas: SIL International, 1988.

> Analyzes the communication roles in Hebrews via discourse analysis. The exegetical notes are informed by solid linguistic theory. This work strives to get at the meaning of the Greek text. Excellent resource!

Westcott, B. F. *The Epistle to the Hebrews: The Greek Text with Notes and Essays*. London: Macmillan, 1892.

> This classic work has stood the test of time and is still rewarding to read. Minute attention to detailed exegesis. Westcott's knowledge of patristic and medieval interpreters in original Greek and Latin is impressive. He employs numerous excurses addressing significant theological issues. I still turn to this work and am never disappointed.

Allen, David L. *Hebrews*. NAC. Nashville: Broadman & Holman, 2010.

> I have attempted to bring discourse analysis to bear on the overall structure of the letter in an effort to exhibit the sentential, paragraph, section, and discourse structure of Hebrews. A verse-by-verse, paragraph-by-paragraph treatment focusing on exegesis, exposition, and theological implications. I have given extensive space to treating the prologue [1:1–4] and the famous warning passage in 6:1–8, the latter extending to 50 pages and to my knowledge is the longest analysis of the various views in a commentary in print. I wrote with pastors in mind. 672 pages. See also the companion volume *Lukan Authorship of Hebrews*. Studies in Bible and Theology. Nashville: Broadman & Holman, 2010, an expansion of my Ph.D. dissertation.

Barclay, William. *The Letter to the Hebrews*. Revised edition. DSB. Philadelphia: Westminster, 1976.

> I would consider this the best of Barclay's volumes in the DSB series. Barclay was a world-renowned Scottish New Testament scholar. His knowledge of Greek is vast, and it shows in this volume. Excellent word studies and illustrations to boot. For example, consider this gem from his treatment of Hebrews in 10:1–2: "Without Christ you cannot get beyond the shadows of God." Buy it!

Bruce, F. F. *The Epistle to the Hebrews*. NICNT. Grand Rapids: Eerdmans, 1997.

> Bruce's volume is still one of my favorites on the epistle. I consider it his best work. It is a slight revision of his 1964 edition, with emphasis on the word "slight." Nevertheless, it has stood the test of time and is very valuable to the expositor.

Cockerill, Gareth Lee. *The Epistle to the Hebrews*. NICNT. Grand Rapids: Eerdmans, 2012.

> Replaces the Bruce volume above. Cockerill writes from the Wesleyan tradition, and this is now probably one of the top five more recent commentaries on Hebrews. Cockerill wrote his Ph.D. dissertation on Melchizedek in Hebrews 7. His work is a good balance to the Reformed commentaries on Hebrews.

Greenlee, J. Harold. *Exegetical Summary of Hebrews*. 2nd ed. Dallas: SIL International, 2008.

> Greenlee, a scholar in textual criticism, was the secretary of the committee for the UBS 3rd edition Greek New Testament. I had the privilege of having him serve as an outside reader for my Ph.D. dissertation on Lukan authorship of Hebrews back in 1987. See Abernathy under Romans for information on books in this series. In my judgment, every pastor should own all volumes in this series. It can be a huge time saver, and it often addresses semantic issues not discussed in other exegetical commentaries.

Guthrie, George H. *Hebrews*. NIVAC. Grand Rapids: Zondervan, 1998.

> One of the best volumes in this series. Guthrie wrote his Ph.D. dissertation at Southwestern Baptist Theological Seminary on the structure of Hebrews. Guthrie's treatment will be of immense help to preachers.

Hughes, Philip Edgcumbe. *A Commentary on the Epistle to the Hebrews*. Grand Rapids: Eerdmans, 1987.

> I read Hughes for his survey of the history of interpretation of the book. This is a good exposition from a Reformed orientation.

O'Brien, Peter T. *The Letter to the Hebrews*. PNTC. Grand Rapids: Eerdmans, 2010.

> This is one of the top five commentaries on Hebrews, especially for pastors. It is readable, exegetical, and expositionally sound. Superb scholarship here from a Reformed perspective. Gives a bit more attention to the thorny passage in Hebrews 6:4–6 than most, but still a slim treatment.

## DEVOTIONAL COMMENTARIES

Griffith Thomas, W. H. *Hebrews: A Devotional Commentary*. Grand Rapids: Eerdmans, 1962.

> Here are 41 devotional messages by one of the premier devotional writers on Scripture.

Meyer, F. B. *The Way into the Holiest: Expositions of Hebrews*. New York: Revell, 1893.

> Meyer, Baptist pastor and contemporary of Spurgeon, met D. L. Moody in 1873, and the two become fast friends. Author of more than 40 books, he is best known for his devotional works and books on Bible characters. This is a warm-hearted devotional work of 35 short meditations on selected passages in Hebrews that should be in every pastor's library.

Murray, Andrew. *The Holiest of All: An Exposition of the Epistle to the Hebrews*. Westwood, NJ: Revell, 1960.

> This 550-page work is a classic! It is the best devotional work on Hebrews. I remember reading Murray late one Saturday night when I was getting ready to preach on Hebrews the next morning. He warms the soul. Consider this gem from 8:12–13: "Pardon is the door, holiness the pathway, and the presence of God the blessing. ... The three blessings: pardon of sin, purity of heart, and the presence of God." Don't forget to read all Murray's books on prayer as well, especially *With Christ in the School of Prayer*. Westwood, NJ: Revell, 1953.

Newell, William. *Hebrews: Verse by Verse*. Grand Rapids: Kregel, 2005.

> Commissioned by D. L. Moody to a teaching ministry shortly before his death, Newell carried on an international teaching ministry until his death in 1956. This is one of the top devotional commentaries on Hebrews. He is also the author of the great hymn "At Calvary."

## SPECIAL STUDIES

Lincoln, Andrew. *Hebrews: A Guide*. London: T&T Clark, 2006.

> Excellent pastoral resource surveying canonical position, genre and rhetoric, structure, background, use of the Old Testament, Christology, soteriology, and eschatology. Very helpful resource.

Trotter, Andrew. *Interpreting the Epistle to the Hebrews*. Grand Rapids: Baker, 1997.

> Out of print but a very helpful volume for the preacher. Covers matters of introduction, structure, textual issues, exegetical issues, and theology in an easy-to-follow manner.

## SERMONS

Draper, James. *Hebrews: The Life that Pleases God*. Wheaton: Tyndale, 1976.

> See above on Titus. These are excellent, practical, down-to-earth sermons that explain the text well. Draper gets the warning passages right to boot!

Manton, Thomas. *By Faith: Sermons on Hebrews 11*. Edinburgh: Banner of Truth, 2000 reprint [1873 edition].

Here are 65 sermons on 31 verses! In typical Puritan fashion, Manton is interested in proclaiming Puritan theology as much as he is the text of Scripture, but these sermons are worth a read if you have time. He is also the author of almost 1,700 pages of sermons on Psalm 119 in three volumes. In fact, 22 volumes of his extant works consist mostly of sermons.

M'Cheyne, Robert Murray. *Sermons on Hebrews*. Michael McMullen, ed. Edinburgh: Banner of Truth, 2004.

At the beginning of the 20th century, James Macdonald of Edinburgh purchased a box of old papers that belonged to a preacher of around 60 years earlier. The contents turned out to be the notebooks and sermon notes of Robert Murray M'Cheyne. Here are 24 sermons on selected paragraphs in Hebrews by the famed pastor in Brighton.

Perkins, William. *A Commentary on Hebrews 11*. New York: Pilgrim Press, 1991 reprint.

This work, originally by one of the greatest of the Puritans, appeared in 1609 and is a series of expositions on Hebrews 11:1–12:1 preached at Cambridge in the 1590s. Worthy of your time if you have time.

Seiss, Joseph A. *Lectures on Hebrews*. Grand Rapids: Baker, 1954.

Here are 36 sermons that will warm your heart. You will find sermonic help for your own preaching here. See Seiss on Revelation as well.

Vines, Jerry. *Hebrews*. Neptune, NJ: Loizeaux, 1993.

Excellent expository sermons from this experienced Baptist pastor and expositor. Vines was pastor of First Baptist Church in Jacksonville, Fla., for 25 years.

# JAMES

## EXEGETICAL COMMENTARIES

Blomberg, Craig L. and Mariam J. Kamell. *James*. ZECNT. Grand Rapids: Zondervan, 2008.

Solid exegesis, theology, and application will benefit all preachers. Strong on the structure of James.

Davids, Peter H. *The Epistle of James*. NIGTC. Grand Rapids: Eerdmans, 1982.

Strong exegetical treatment, extensive discussion of theology, and pays attention to the literary structure and flow of argument. Concern for theology and pastoral issues make it useful for teaching and preaching, says Bauer

Martin, Ralph. *James*. WBC. Waco, TX: Word, 1988.

Strong and accurate exegetical analysis informed by Martin's extensive knowledge of ancient and modern literature. Denies James' authorship and argues his disciples arranged sayings of James into this letter. "A masterpiece of condensed learning," says Carson. A good, solid treatment that would benefit serious scholars/pastors.

Mayor, Joseph. *The Epistle of St. James: The Greek Text with Introduction and Comments*. 2nd ed. Grand Rapids: Baker, 1978.

One of the top technical commentaries on James ever produced. More than 500 pages, with 260 of those dealing with introductory material. This will be too much and too difficult for pastors without knowledge of Greek. Mayor was professor of classics at Kings College in London and then honorary fellow of St. John's College in Cambridge.

McCartney, Dan G. *James*. BECNT. Grand Rapids: Baker, 2009.

"Contains rigorous exegesis and carefully worded and probing theological reflection," says Carson.

Vlachos, Chris. *James: Exegetical Guide to the Greek New Testament*. Nashville: Broadman & Holman, 2013.

Pastors will find this volume, and all in this series, very helpful in their exegetical spadework for sermon preparation. Carson calls it a stellar volume, containing information on important exegetical options. Don't miss the homiletical hints as well.

Greenlee, J. Harold. *Exegetical Summary of James*. Dallas: SIL International, 1993.

See under Hebrews above.

Guthrie, George. *James*. REBC 13. Grand Rapids: Zondervan, 2006.

Guthrie is a solid exegete who is always helpful to the pastor when he writes.

Hiebert, D. Edmond. *James*. Revised ed. Chicago: Moody, 1992.

As the reader has noticed many times in this survey, Hiebert always gets high marks from me. He writes with expository preachers in mind. You cannot afford to miss him.

Johnson, Luke Timothy. *The Letter of James*. AB. New Haven: Yale University Press, 2008.

Bauer says it is arguably the best commentary on James, calling it "lucid, elegantly written, and theologically profound." Johnson offers the most comprehensive survey of the history of interpretation of the book to be found in English. Good analysis of the relationship of James to the rest of the New Testament, especially Paul. Emphasizes linguistic analysis and the overall coherent structure of the book. This is one of the better volumes in the Anchor series.

McKnight, Scot. *The Letter of James*. NICNT. Grand Rapids: Eerdmans, 2011.

McKnight weighs in at almost 500 pages. "Written with verve and clarity ... a cornucopia of learning and reflection," says Carson.

Moo, Douglas J. *The Letter of James*. PNTC. Grand Rapids: Eerdmans, 2000.

"A lovely blend of good judgment, good writing, good theology, and sometimes good application," says Carson.

Vaughan, Curtis. *James*. Cape Coral, FL: Founders Press, 2003.

Originally from the Study Guide Series and published in 1969, this is a brief but helpful treatment of the letter that would benefit pastors, especially those without any Greek training. Vaughan was the venerable professor of New Testament and Greek at Southwestern Seminary for almost 40 years.

## DEVOTIONAL COMMENTARIES

Blanchard, John. *Truth for Life: A Devotional Commentary on the Epistle of James.* 2nd ed. Durham, England: Evangelical Press, 1986.

Blanchard is an internationally known evangelist who has written numerous best-selling books. This commentary is primarily devotional, but it is based on exposition of the text. The preacher will find lots of help here.

Manton, Thomas. *An Exposition of the Epistle of James.* London: Banner of Truth, 1968.

A devotional classic. Wordy—in the Puritan tradition (don't dare preach this way!)—but full of application.

Zodhiates, Spiros. *The Behavior of Belief: An Exposition of James Based upon the Original Greek Text.* 3 volumes in one. Ridgefield, NJ: AMG Press, 1966 (Originally published by Eerdmans in a one-volume edition).

A Greek by birth, Zodhiates' work is very helpful for providing illustrations and application, combined with some good word studies, for the pastor. He is not, however, up on advances in Greek studies that have occurred over the past 40 years.

## SPECIAL STUDIES

Chester, Andrew and Ralph Martin. *The Theology of the Letters of James, Peter, and Jude.* Cambridge: Cambridge University Press, 1994.

Part of the New Testament Theology series, this work provides a brief but helpful overview of the theology of these letters. Chester deals with James; Martin with 1 and 2 Peter and Jude. Pastors will find this work and all works in this series helpful, though they will find some theological disagreement along the way.

Taylor, Mark. *A Text-linguistic Investigation into the Discourse Structure of James.* London: T&T Clark, 2006.

Taylor teaches New Testament and Greek at Southwestern Baptist Theological Seminary. This is the fruit of his Ph.D. dissertation. It is important since there has been such disagreement about the structure of James. This will aid preachers in determining how to preach the paragraph units of the book.

Dale, R. W. *The Epistle of James and Other Discourses*. London: Hodder & Stoughton, 1895.

Ten sermons covering material through James 4:1–6 and 10 additional miscellaneous sermons from the great pastor in Birmingham, England. Dale made copious use of Mayor's commentary on James (see above) in the preparation of these sermons.

Stier, Rudolph. *The Epistle of St. James*. Minneapolis: Klock & Klock, 1982.

From the mind and heart of a German scholar/pastor who exhibited the best of 19th-century German pietism comes this series of expository sermons delivered to his church. Here is exposition and application co-mingled in a helpful way to contemporary pastors.

# 1 PETER

## EXEGETICAL COMMENTARIES

Forbes, Greg. *1 Peter*. EGGNT. Nashville: Broadman & Holman, 2014.

Michael Bird says, "Forbes has produced a thick reading ... that is an exegetical gold mine." Carson says it well: "Forbes provides, in succinct form, the wealth of exegetical detail that pastors and students want and need but often do not have time to amass for themselves."

Jobes, Karen H. *1 Peter*. BECNT. Grand Rapids: Baker, 2005.

Jobes is the Gerald F. Hawthorne Professor of New Testament Greek and Exegesis at Wheaton College. She was converted in college when someone gave her a copy of Hal Lindsey's *Late Great Planet Earth* and a copy of the new NIV gospel of John. A Septuagint scholar, Jobes brings her knowledge of the Greek Old Testament to bear upon her work. This work deftly incorporates rhetorical and social-scientific methodologies with traditional exegesis. Scholarly yet workmanlike for the pastor.

Johnstone, Robert. *The First Epistle of Peter: Revised Text with Introduction and Commentary*. Minneapolis: James Family Christian Publishers, 1978 reprint [1888].

Johnstone's work not only treats the epistle exegetically but also attempts to tie together the sections of the letter into a coherent whole—something that was not always done in 19th-century commentaries. Johnstone carefully weighs alternative interpretations (see his treatment of 4:17, for example). Conservative and worth your time.

## EXPOSITORY COMMENTARIES

Davids, Peter H. *The First Epistle of Peter*. NICNT. Grand Rapids: Eerdmans, 1990.

Good analysis of literary structure with a focus on theology. Less focused on linguistic analysis or historical background. This volume is useful for preachers.

Hiebert, D. Edmond. *First Peter: An Expositional Commentary*. Chicago: Moody, 1984.

Thorough exposition, detailed outlines, practical application, and suggested bibliography all converge to make this an especially good commentary for expository preachers. If Hiebert wrote on it, I try to read it.

Kelly, J. N. D. *A Commentary on the Epistles of Peter and of Jude*. BNTC. Grand Rapids: Baker, 1993.

See above under Pastoral Epistles. Originally published in the Blacks NTC series. "In terms of overall serviceability and for the purpose of getting to the heart of Peter's message, J. N. D. Kelly is without peer," says Martin.

Leighton, Robert. *Commentary on First Peter*. Grand Rapids: Kregel, 1972 reprint [1853].

This is Leighton's principal work. Leighton was a 17th-century principle and professor of divinity at the University of Edinburgh and then Archbishop of Glasgow in 1670. He was said to have "a sublime strain in preaching, with so great a gesture and such a majesty, both of thought, of language ... that I never once saw a wandering eye where he preached and have seen whole assemblies often melt in tears before him." Orme said of this volume: "There is learning without its parade, theology divested of systematic stiffness, and eloquence in a beautiful flow of unaffected language and appropriate imagery."

Lillie, John. *Lectures on the First and Second Epistles of Peter*. Minneapolis: Klock & Klock, 1978 reprint [1869].

Though dated, still a worthy tome on Peter's letters. Lillie was a classical and biblical scholar who could glide with ease from a technical Greek exegetical point to a pertinent quote from Oecumenius and then to Shakespeare, all in the same breath (see his comments on 1 Peter 3:1–2). Lillie died in his prime at the age of 55 while pastor of the First Presbyterian Church in Kingston, N.Y. Works like this are so often overlooked by preachers today, yet there is a wealth of treasure in volumes like this.

Marshall, I. Howard. *1 Peter*. IVPNTC. Downers Grove: InterVarsity, 1991.

Carson calls it "superb." Marshall almost always delivers. This is a helpful volume for the preacher.

Michaels, J. Ramsey. *1 Peter*. WBC. Waco, TX: Word, 1988.

The focus is on historical background and lexical and syntactical analysis, but little attention is given to the history of interpretation and application. A solid work overall.

Patterson, Paige. *A Pilgrim Priesthood: An Exposition of the Epistle of First Peter*. Eugene, OR: Wipf & Stock, 2004.

Patterson is president of Southwestern Baptist Theological Seminary and former president of the Southern Baptist Convention. Marvelous, concise, but meaty exposition of the letter. His 20-page treatment of the spirits in prison passage is the best in print.

Schreiner, Thomas R. *1 & 2 Peter and Jude*. NAC. Nashville: Broadman & Holman, 2003.

Carson calls this volume one of the most impressive in the series. He says, "Exegesis and theological reflection couched in admirable clarity." Schreiner teaches New Testament at Southern Seminary and writes from a strongly Reformed soteriological perspective.

Selwyn, E. G. *The First Epistle of St. Peter*. London: Macmillan & Co., 1964.

A hefty volume of 500 pages, chock full of learned exegesis and helpful. "Additional Notes," followed by two lengthy "Essays," the first of which deals with the spirits in prison passage (Selwyn wrongly thinks it refers to the theology of baptism and the Christian life). Only pastors who want to go deeper will ultimately benefit from this volume.

Vaughan, Curtis and Thomas Lea. *1, 2 Peter, Jude*. BSC. Grand Rapids: Zondervan, 1988.

See Romans above on Vaughan. Lea was Professor of New Testament and later dean of the school of theology at Southwestern Seminary. True to the series' intent, this is an excellent volume for pastors, especially those who have no Greek background. The exposition is succinct and on target.

## DEVOTIONAL COMMENTARIES

Jowett, J. H. *The Epistles of St. Peter*. Grand Rapids: Kregel, 1970 reprint [1905].

Jowett was an English Congregationalist educated at Edinburgh and Oxford and who pastored all of his life. He followed R. W. Dale in Birmingham, England, and remained as pastor almost 15 years. For eight years, he pastored New York's famous Fifth Avenue Presbyterian Church. Returning to England, he assumed the pastorate of the famous Westminster Chapel in London, preceding the great G. Campbell Morgan. Jowett's work on Peter's letters is an excellent blend of exposition and application. Verse by verse, even phrase by phrase, Jowett treats us to an expositional/devotional feast. Don't miss this volume.

Meyer, F. B. *Tried by Fire*. New York: Revell, n.d.

Very good devotional work from the pen of this British Baptist. I try to own everything by Meyer.

Lloyd-Jones, David Martyn. *Expository Sermons on Peter*. Carlisle, PA: Banner of Truth, 1983.

These sermons were preached at Westminster Chapel in 1946–47, shortly after Lloyd-Jones became senior pastor. This is his first series of sermons through a book of the Bible. Chosen because of the post-war struggles of his people.

# 2 PETER AND JUDE

## EXEGETICAL COMMENTARIES

Green, Gene L. *Jude and 2 Peter*. BECNT. Grand Rapids: Baker, 2008.

> Substantive, exegetical detail, but still highly accessible to pastors. Green is professor of New Testament at Wheaton. Bauckham says it is "full of careful historical exegesis that is especially well informed by the literature, philosophy, and rhetoric of the Greco-Roman world."

Mayor, Joseph. *The Epistle of St. Jude and the Second Epistle of St. Peter*. Grand Rapids: Baker, 1979 [1907].

> Too detailed and technical for most pastors, but a brilliant exegetical treatment. Latin and Greek quotations and citations from ancient sources abound. Mayor wrongly concludes that 2 Peter is a pseudonymous 2nd-century writing. Mayor was professor of classics at Kings College, London, and then honorary fellow of St. John's College, Cambridge.

## EXPOSITIONAL COMMENTARIES

Bauckham, Richard. *Jude, 2 Peter*. WBC. Nashville: Thomas Nelson, 1983.

> Considers 2 Peter to be pseudepigraphical toward the end of the 1st century, but Bauckham's work is a serious treatment of the literary and syntactical structure and theology. He is also strong on the history of interpretation for interested readers. Bauer said of it in 2003: "The most authoritative and current commentary on these books." Carson considers it the best commentary on these letters.

Davids, Peter H. *The Letters of 2 Peter and Jude*. PNTC. Grand Rapids: Eerdmans, 2006.

> Rich exegesis and thoughtful theological reflection according to Carson. A helpful volume to pastors.

Green, Michael. *The Second General Epistle of Peter and the General Epistle of Jude*. TNTC. 2nd ed. Grand Rapids: Eerdmans, 2007.

> Green is an Oxford theologian and Anglican priest who has authored more than 50 books. One of his most important, which should be in every pastor's library, is *Evangelism in the Early Church*. This work is solid and accessible to any pastor. A worthy investment.

Hiebert, D. Edmond. *Second Peter and Jude: An Expositional Commentary*. Greenville, SC: BJU, 1989.

Hiebert calls these epistles "the dark corner of the New Testament." He shines a bright light on these treasures, helping preachers to share the gems with their congregations. Excellent exposition with strong focus on application makes this volume valuable to the expositor. I own everything Hiebert has written.

Manton, Thomas. *An Exposition on the Epistle of Jude*. Wilmington, DE: Sovereign Grace Publishers, 1972.

This is considered a classic by the prolific Puritan. Though old, it is still worth your perusal.

Moo, Douglas J. *2 Peter, Jude*. NIVAC. Grand Rapids: Zondervan, 1997.

Moo's volume is strong on exposition but then moves to application. Very helpful to the expository preacher.

Schreiner, Thomas R. *1 & 2 Peter and Jude*. NAC. Nashville: Broadman & Holman, 2003.

See above on 1 Peter.

Vaughan, Curtis and Thomas Lea. *1, 2 Peter, Jude*. BSC. Grand Rapids: Zondervan, 1988.

See on Romans above.

# 1, 2, 3 JOHN

## EXEGETICAL COMMENTARIES

Anderson, John. *An Exegetical Summary of 1, 2, and 3 John*. Dallas: SIL International, 1992.

For this series, see above under Romans. I consider the volumes in this series indispensable for the working pastor. Collates material from numerous commentaries, lexicons, and Bible translations and presents them in a succinct fashion. Informed by solid linguistic theory, Anderson is interested in the semantic structure of the letters of John. Preachers will find invaluable help here.

Culy, Martin. *I, II, III John: A Handbook on the Greek Text*. Waco, TX: Baylor University Press, 2005.

From a trained linguist, preachers will find this brief volume very helpful. Treats the book paragraph by paragraph, with excellent exegetical notations, followed by a helpful bibliography.

Plummer, Alfred. *The Epistles of St. John*. Grand Rapids: Baker, 1980 reprint [1886].

Plummer wrote commentaries on more than 15 New Testament books. Based carefully on the Greek text, this is an exegetical gem. Eighty-eight pages of introduction, nine appendices, and almost 200 pages of commentary. First published in the Cambridge Greek Testament for Schools and Colleges. A solid, conservative work that has been somewhat superseded by more modern works but still helpful.

Smalley, Stephen. *1, 2, 3 John*. WBC. Waco, TX: Word, 2007.

Meticulous lexical and semantic analysis of every phrase with attention to the flow of the argument. Also a strong focus on theological meaning. Carson says Smalley is at his best when he is summarizing and interacting with the positions of others.

Westcott, B. F. *The Epistles of St. John: The Greek Text with Notes and Essays*. London: Macmillan, 1883.

Westcott's knowledge of Greek combined with his knowledge of the Church Fathers and classical antiquity is everywhere evident in this volume. This is a standard, classic work.

Yarbrough, Robert W. *1–3 John*. BECNT. Grand Rapids: Baker, 2008.

This is the best overall exegetical/expository work on the letters. A judicious treatment from a recognized New Testament scholar. I used it heavily when writing my volume on 1–3 John in Crossway's *Preaching the Word* series. This is a must-have for preaching the Johannine letters.

Akin, Daniel L. *1, 2, 3 John*. NAC. Nashville: Broadman & Holman, 2001.

From the pen of the president of Southeastern Baptist Theological Seminary, this is one of the best expository commentaries on John's letters available. It is soundly exegetical and expositional with attention to theology as well. I used this volume heavily when preparing my own sermons on 1–3 John in Crossway's *Preaching the Word* series. All preachers should own this one. Akin and I were in college, seminary, and Ph.D. work together.

Burdick, Donald. *The Letters of John the Apostle*. Chicago: Moody, 1985.

This was one of the first commentaries on John's letters I used when preaching through the book in the mid-1980s, and I still find it useful today. Ninety pages of introduction are followed by almost 400 pages of exposition based on the Greek text. Burdick divides the commentary into four sections: exegetical, paraphrastic, structural, and theological. Preachers should consult this volume when preaching through John's letters. Burdick was professor of New Testament at Denver Seminary.

Hiebert, D. Edmond. *The Epistles of John: An Expositional Commentary*. Greenville, SC: Bob Jones University Press, 1991.

From the pen of a noted author, teacher, and commentator, this is one of my favorites on 1 John. Excellent for the expository preacher. Hiebert is clear, conservative, and almost always on target.

Kruse, Colin G. *The Letters of John*. PNTC. Grand Rapids: Eerdmans, 2000.

From the pen of this ordained Anglican minister and New Testament scholar comes a commentary I would probably rank in the top five modern commentaries on John's letters. A verse-by-verse treatment that is attuned to the important theological issues. Good combination of scholarship and spiritual insight. Kruse authored the Romans volume in the Pillar series released in 2012.

Law, Robert. *The Tests of Life: A Study of the First Epistle of St. John*. 3rd ed. Grand Rapids: Baker, 1979 [reprint of 1914 edition].

Law was professor of New Testament literature and exegesis at Knox College, Toronto. Most consider this a classic on 1 John. Technically, this is not a commentary, but it provides more exegetical insight than some commentaries according to Scholer. More doctrinal in orientation, the book attempts a thorough analysis of John's teaching. "A devotional classic and a seed plot of many sermons," says Martin. Don't leave home without this one!

Lias, John. *An Exposition of the First Epistle of John*. Minneapolis: Klock & Klock, 1982 [1887].

> Though the exposition is based on the Greek text, this worthy work is written for pastors. Each chapter of this book appeared serially in the *Homiletic Magazine*. Treats the text and application in a masterful fashion. Highly recommended.

Marshall, I. Howard. *The Epistles of John*. NICNT. Grand Rapids: Eerdmans, 1978.

> Here again is vintage Marshall. Not a lengthy volume but chock full of meaty stuff. Bauer says it is "characterized by careful argumentation, balanced judgment, and clear and understandable presentation of current scholarly discussions of complex exegetical issues." Preachers will benefit from it.

Stott, John. *The Letters of John*. TNTC. 2nd ed. Grand Rapids: Eerdmans, 2007.

> Exegesis, exposition, and application blended together as only Stott can do it. Own and read everything he writes.

Thatcher, Tom. *1–3 John*. REBC 13. Grand Rapids: Zondervan, 2006.

> Glynn was the proofreader for this entire volume and said Thatcher's treatment of John's letters was the best.

## DEVOTIONAL COMMENTARIES

Griffith Thomas, W. H. *The Apostle John: Studies in His Life and Writings*. Grand Rapids: Eerdmans, 1968.

> Covers the life of John, the Gospel, the letters, and Revelation. Griffith Thomas is known as a superb devotional writer. His works are well worth your investment.

## SERMONS

Allen, David L. *1–3 John: Fellowship in God's Family*. PTW. Wheaton: Crossway, 2013.

> Twenty sermons as I would preach them from the pulpit on the Greek paragraphs of 1 John, followed by one sermon each on 2 and 3 John. Each sermon contains extensive footnotes so pastors can see where I acquired some of the exegetical, expositional, or illustrative material in the sermon. Hence I refer to them as "sermontaries." This is my attempt at practicing what I preach: text-driven preaching.

Candlish, Robert. *The Epistle of John Expounded in a Series of Lectures*. London: Banner of Truth, 1973.

Candlish was principal of New College and pastor of Free St. George's Church, Edinburgh. "Some pages here seem to be almost perfect. The book will search one's heart, it will lift him up into new heights," says Wilbur Smith.

Stedman, Ray. *Expository Studies in 1 John: Life by the Son*. Waco, TX: Word, 1980.

Stedman was the pastor of Peninsula Bible Church in Palo Alto, Calif., for many years. He was a gifted expositor with a practical focus, much like Charles Swindoll. His works are very useful for preaching.

Vines, Jerry. *Exploring 1, 2, 3 John*. Neptune, NJ: Loizeaux, 1989.

Excellent sermons from the preaching ministry of one of Southern Baptists' premier expositors. I was called to preach under his preaching ministry in 1973. Vines is the single most influential person on my own preaching ministry. Paige Patterson said of this work: "There are many good preachers. There are many good theologians. Rare is the opportunity to read a genuinely good commentary like this one by a genuinely adroit pastor-theologian."

# REVELATION

## EXEGETICAL COMMENTARIES

Aune, David. *Revelation*. WBC. 3 volumes. Dallas: Word, 1997–1998.

> This is the most massive commentary on Revelation, weighing in at more than 1,350 pages. The introduction alone is 250 pages. Engages in unnecessary redaction-criticism, is highly technical, and is lacking in theological analysis but covers the linguistic, literary, historical, and every other waterfront with encyclopedic treatment. This will be too heavy for many pastors, but some will want to consult it.

Beale, G. K. *The Book of Revelation*. NIGTC. Grand Rapids: Eerdmans, 1998.

> Beale's work must be reckoned as one of the top commentaries on the apocalypse. This is a comprehensive treatment of the book. Focuses on the use of the Old Testament in Jewish exegetical traditions as key to the book. Strong on historical background and careful attention to the argument. Occasionally dense prose. Amillennial perspective. No one agrees completely with any commentator on Revelation, but one cannot afford to neglect what Beale says.

Osborne, Grant R. *Revelation*. BECNT. Grand Rapids: Baker, 2002.

> True to form, Osborne has written a solid exegetical/expositional commentary on Revelation.

Thomas, Robert. *Revelation 1–7: An Exegetical Commentary*. WEC. Chicago: Moody, 1992.

> An excellent exegetical treatment. Thomas interprets the book in a premillennial, pretribulational fashion.

_____. *Revelation 8–22: An Exegetical Commentary*. WEC. Chicago: Moody, 1995.

> See above.

## EXPOSITORY COMMENTARIES

Keener, Craig S. *Revelation*. NIVAC. Grand Rapids: Zondervan, 2000.

> Keener is most helpful to the preacher on the issue of application.

Mounce, Robert H. *Revelation*. NICNT. Rev. ed. Grand Rapids: Eerdmans, 1997.

Mounce's work is well worth your time. Those with little or no background in Greek will benefit from this volume, as will all others. Premillennial perspective. I would consult it if preaching through Revelation.

Patterson, Paige. *Revelation*. NAC. Nashville: Broadman & Holman, 2012.

This is Patterson's magnum opus, the fruit of years of study and preaching from the apocalypse. Thoroughly sound exegesis, exposition, application, and thoroughly premillennial. Those with a different eschatology should not ignore this important commentary. Expositors cannot afford to be without it.

Phillips, John. *Exploring Revelation*. Chicago: Moody, 1974.

Expositors will glean lots of helpful exposition, illustrations, and applications, not to mention outlines, from Phillips. Premillennial perspective.

Walvoord, John. *The Revelation of Jesus Christ*. Chicago: Moody, 1966.

This is an older but very solid premillennial treatment of Revelation from the former president of Dallas Theological Seminary. Probably his best work. Readable, clear, concise, but meaty treatment.

## SPECIAL STUDIES

Michaels, J. Ramsey. *Interpreting the Book of Revelation*. Grand Rapids: Baker, 1992.

This volume is part of the *Guides to New Testament Exegesis* series, some of which are out of print. Provides a concise introduction to issues of genre, authorship, historical and social setting, and structure, followed by chapters on text criticism, grammar and style, narrative criticism, tradition history, and theological interpretation. Regardless of one's own take concerning Revelation, this is a very helpful volume.

## SERMONS

Criswell, W. A. *Expository Sermons on Revelation*. Grand Rapids: Zondervan, 1966.

These excellent sermons represent the very best from Criswell, the famed pastor of First Baptist Church in Dallas, Texas, from 1944 until 1994. Criswell preached through books of the Bible in his church. Premillennial perspective. This is a volume you cannot afford to be without when preaching through Revelation.

Seiss, Joseph A. *The Apocalypse: A Series of Special Lectures on the Revelation of Jesus Christ*. New York: Cosimo, 2007 reprint.

Originally published in 1865, it has been reprinted numerous times. Smith calls it the most famous expository work in our language (1939): "There is no man in the English world today ... a pastor of a church as Seiss was, who is equipped both with a knowledge of the Word and a gift of oratory, to deliver such a series of lectures as these."